Bread and Freedom

Basic human needs and human rights

John Grindle

TRÓCAIRE
and
GILL and MACMILLAN

Published in Ireland by

TRÓCAIRE

Catholic Agency for World Development
169 Booterstown Ave.,
Blackrock, Co. Dublin
and
Gill and Macmillan Ltd,
Goldenbridge, Inchicore, Dublin 8
with associated companies in
Auckland, Budapest, Gaborone, Harare, Hong Kong,
Kampala, Kuala Lumpur, Lagos, London, Madras, Manzini,
Melbourne, Mexico City, Nairobi, New York, Singapore,
Sydney, Tokyo, Windhoek

© Trócaire 1992
ISBN O 7171 1967 X

Design: The Graphiconies
Print origination by Typeform Ltd
Printed in Ireland by Genprint

A catalogue record is available for this book from the British
Library.

Contents

TABLES

Foreword

The wave of natural and man-made disasters sweeping over the Third World during 1991 could not but induce a sense of despair. It seemed that the most we could hope for was damage limitation, while objectives of longer-term development appeared hopelessly unrealistic.

Indeed, many of the statistics of recent years suggest that poverty has worsened. The debt crisis of the 1980s contributed to falling incomes and cut-backs in services for millions of people. More frequent wars have led to heightened insecurity – the number of refugees doubled in the 1980s.

Against this background, John Grindle's study is especially timely. He points out that despite the economic problems of the 1980s, progress in human development was still made. For example, the proportion of children vaccinated against the six main vaccine-preventable diseases has been increased from under 10% to over 50% in the past decade, thus saving the lives of 1.5 million children annually. Similarly, the proportion of children with diarrhoea being treated with oral rehydration therapy has increased from under 1% in 1980 to almost 25%, saving approximately one million lives each year. Far too many people still suffer from malnutrition, illness and poverty, but these achievements are significant and deserve to be acknowledged as such.

Bread and Freedom places these recent trends in a context of longer-term advances in the provision of basic needs. Life expectancy in the Third World has increased by 50% since 1950, an increase which the currently industrialised countries took two centuries to achieve. Around 60% of adults in the developing countries are now literate, compared with only one third in 1950. Over the same period, under-5 mortality has been cut by half. Primary education has become almost universal, and the proportion of the relevant age group attending secondary school has almost trebled since 1960.

Progress of this sort is uneven, both in terms of indicators (the numbers of malnourished are increasing) and in terms of regions (Sub-Saharan Africa has fared worse then elsewhere). But this study cautions us against the counsel of despair which would have us believe that all attempts to improve the human condition are futile. Progress *is* possible and it *has* been achieved.

Equally, this progress should not become an excuse for complacency. John Grindle also points out that despite continuing progress, up to one quarter of the people of the Third World will not have enough income to meet their basic needs in the year 2000. In that year, 600 million people will still lack the most basic need of all, adequate food. This situation can be rectified – low-cost solutions have been tried and tested, and they could be implemented quickly if the political will was mobilised. An outlay of $30-$50 billion per annum would allow the most essential human needs of every person on the planet to be fulfilled by the year 2000. This sum is around 5% of the annual military expenditure; no new resources need be generated, only new priorities.

But *Bread and Freedom* goes beyond arguing for some kind of global welfare exercise, necessary as that obviously is. John Grindle also argues for a strategy which would foster the development of human rights as well as the fulfillment of human needs. In fact, it is useful to view basic needs as 'economic rights' which should carry the same moral and legal force as political and civil rights. These two sets of rights reinforce each other; it is those countries where political and civil rights are respected which tend to also record the best performances on indicators such as life expectancy, infant survival and average income. John Grindle argues that this finding should not be surprising; human rights are indivisible, whether classified as economic or political. In the absence of basic civil and political rights, the full participation of people in their own development is blocked, thus limiting their access to their economic rights. At the same time, basic economic and social rights allow people to enjoy their civil and political freedoms. Progress must be made on all fronts together.

One of the most important conclusions of this study is that "the emergence of thousands of voluntary human rights and development groups in Third World countries is the single most important contemporary force working for increased global respect for international humanitarian principles. The main emphasis of Northern NGOs should be on building up the capacity of local NGOs, while campaigning at home and abroad for the indivisibility of human rights, whether political or economic". This is exactly the type of work which Trócaire carries out: supporting indigenous self-help projects overseas, and raising awareness at home about the causes of poverty and promoting the rights of the marginalised. John Grindle's study not only contributes to that work, it also provides it with a solid intellectual underpinning.

Brian McKeown,
Director,
Trócaire,
Dublin, 1992

8

Preface

I am grateful to Trócaire for giving me the opportunity to undertake this study, as I have felt for some time that the very real achievements in relation to basic needs in the Third World were not getting due recognition. The rate of progress in developing countries in this respect is far in advance of that achieved by the currently industrialised countries at similar stages of development.

This is not to understate the high level of deprivation in relation to both material needs and human rights which is still to be found in all too many countries. However, by focussing only on deprivation and ignoring achievements, development agencies and commentators may inadvertently spread a gospel of despair, while the past progress and newer technologies provide a basis for hope.

Another theme in this study is the indivisibility of human rights, whether classified as civil and political or economic and social. In the absence of basic civil and political rights, the full participation of people in their own development and empowerment is blocked, thus limiting their capacity to gain their entitlement to economic rights. On the other hand, it is the economic and social rights which allow people to enjoy their civil and political freedoms.

The study was supported and guided by the Trócaire Research Advisors, Mary Sutton and later Andy Storey, for whose assistance and gentle pressure I am very grateful. The members of the Research Advisory Group, Alan Matthews, Frank Barry, Patrick Commins, Tony Fahey, Connell Fanning and Eoin O'Malley, read drafts of the study and made valuable comments. I owe a particular debt to the two librarians who ensured access to the large body of material reviewed, namely Anne Kinsella in Trócaire and Mary Riordan in the Development Studies Library in University College, Dublin.

As befalls all authors, I must accept responsibility for the views expressed and any errors or misinterpretations.

John Grindle
January 1992

Executive Summary

CHAPTER ONE: The Development Context
This chapter sets the scene for the subsequent analysis, by examining long-term trends in economic growth, poverty and financial (including aid) flows. There have been examples of rapid growth amongst many different kinds of economies, but little absolute increase in incomes per head in the poorest countries. The proportion of people in poverty has been reduced but, with rapid population growth, there has only been a modest reduction in the numbers of the poor. Aid flows (in real terms) stagnated in the 1980s, while there has been a shift of emphasis towards aid to Africa. However, there is no clear relationship between aid allocations and the basic needs records of recipient countries.

CHAPTER TWO: The Basic Needs Approach to Development
By the early 1970s, there was increasing concern about the distribution of the benefits of economic growth. This led to the "enthronement" of basic needs at the World Employment Conference in 1976, with the objective of satisfying the essential requirements of each country's population by the year 2000.

The basic needs approach dominated development thinking in the late 1970s and was a major influence on the policies of donor agencies. In the 1980s, the emphasis shifted from growth to "adjustment"; the UNICEF concept of "Adjustment With a Human Face" added a poverty alleviation dimension to adjustment in the same way as basic needs added such a dimension to growth.

Basic needs is an approach to development, not a single strategy; it sets objectives but does not dictate the means to achieve them. It differs from other approaches in focussing on consumption and giving primary attention to the role of public goods. It also represents an explicit departure from conventional assumptions about consumer sovereignty, as it involves selecting certain types of goods for special attention.

It has been alternatively interpreted as a revolutionary approach, calling for radical redistribution, and as a minimal welfare package to keep the poor quiet and thus avoid radical reforms.

CHAPTER THREE: Trends in Provision of Basic Needs
Life expectancy in developing countries has increased by about half since 1950, an achievement which took two centuries in the

presently industrialised countries. Almost 60% of adults in the developing world are now literate, compared with one third in 1950; under-5 mortality has been halved, with substantial progress in all regions. Food availability has improved in most areas, with a consequent decline in the proportion under-nourished, but an increase in the absolute numbers. Primary education is becoming almost universal and the proportion of the relevant age group attending secondary school has almost trebled since 1960. China has recorded the most dramatic progress on most indicators, while Sub-Saharan Africa has lagged behind.

However, a number of indicators suggest increasing insecurity in the Third World, e.g. the number of natural disasters and the frequency of wars has increased. One of the consequences has been the doubling of the number of refugees during the past decade. Over half of all developing countries are under military rule, compared to one-quarter in 1960.

Despite the economic problems of the 1980s, progress was still recorded on most basic needs indicators – but at a slower rate than previously. Of particular note are the continuing advances in primary health care, so that the proportion of children immunised against the six main vaccine-preventable diseases increased from under 10% to over 50% in the 1980s. However, some 14 million children in the developing world are still dying each year from common illnesses and malnutrition.

CHAPTER FOUR: Factors Affecting Performance on Basic Needs
The most important variable explaining the average level of basic needs satisfaction is average income—as material basic needs are ultimately satisfied out of material income—but the connection is not invariable. Thus countries like China and Sri Lanka have achieved high levels of life expectancy and low under-5 mortality rates at per capita income levels of $300-400, while Brazil and Mexico, with average per capita incomes over five times as high, are still far short of such basic needs levels. At lower levels of income, economic growth appears to be necessary for progress on basic needs; at higher income levels, distributional factors play the major role. At any rate, there is no evidence of any conflict between basic needs achievement and economic growth or industrialisation. Thus, it is possible to meet the more pressing basic needs, even at fairly low levels of income, without sacrificing economic growth.

Countries can meet basic needs in a variety of ways, but well-directed public expenditure is an essential component of all strategies. It has been estimated that it would have taken Sri Lanka up to 150 years to achieve its current high level of life expectancy primarily through growth, rather than through direct public action. In all analyses, basic education emerged as the top sectoral priority, with female education being especially significant.

The argument that poor nations cannot afford the luxury of civil and political rights is belied by their own experience, as those countries whose citizens enjoyed greater political and civil rights also performed better in terms of life expectancy, infant survival rates and per capita incomes. Economic and social rights in turn put people in a position to implement civil and political freedom for themselves.

The battle between the direct (basic needs) and the indirect (via income) approach to poverty alleviation is giving way to an emerging consensus that both are important and, indeed, complementary. However, a harmony of interests between human resource developers and humanitarians cannot be taken for granted in all cases.

CHAPTER FIVE: Basic Needs and Human Rights
The two Covenants (on Civil/Political and Economic/Social/ Cultural Rights), which translate the Universal Declaration of Human Rights into enforceable legal norms, are now accepted by the majority of UN members. Ireland ratified these covenants towards the end of 1989.

Basic needs could be a mechanism for promoting the broader concept of economic, social and cultural rights. Thus, the right to life may be seen as a positive right, requiring action by others, as well as a negative right requiring merely non-interference. Such a right would also imply correlative obligations, on national states and on the international community.

Reliance on the market to allocate all goods and services would imply a value-judgement that the satisfaction of anyone's preferences takes priority over the satisfaction of everyone's basic needs. Thus, there is a need to supplement the market mechanism by public action to ensure minimal levels of basic goods and services for all.

The basic needs concept yields a criterion for selecting a core of "basic rights" which, if fulfilled, could assure a minimal threshold of well-being. This approach could be made operational by means of country-specific thresholds, measured by indicators such as infant mortality, nutrition, income, etc. for different socio-economic groups.

International enforcement of economic, social and cultural rights depends mainly on publicity associated with the reporting system, but this can significantly influence other countries' policies towards the deviant state. There is a need for evaluative criteria (and disaggregated data) for assessing states' activities, e.g. human impact statements analogous to currently popular environmental impact statements. Donors should incorporate human rights considerations in their development policies and monitor them on a regular basis.

The emergence of thousands of voluntary human rights and development groups in Third World countries is the single most important contemporary force working for increased global respect for international humanitarian principles. The main emphasis of Northern NGOs should be on building up the capacity of local NGOs, while campaigning at home and abroad for the acceptance of the indivisibility of human rights, whether political or economic.

CHAPTER SIX: Basic Needs Prospects and Policy Challenges
Despite substantial past and continuing progress, the projections indicate that up to one-quarter of the developing world's population will still have inadequate incomes to meet their basic needs in the year 2000; around half of that number (600 million people) will lack the most basic need, adequate food.

Large-scale action in all the main areas of basic needs is now possible at reasonable cost, as they are susceptible to low-cost solutions which have already been tried and tested. The additional financial resources required to meet the most essential human needs by the year 2000 would be $30-$50 billion per year, i.e. around 5% of today's military spending. If external aid were to meet half the cost, it would have to increase by 50%, while ensuring that at least one-third of the total was allocated to meeting the basic needs of the poorest groups. If this were to be more than a large-scale welfare exercise, it must also involve the creation of conditions conducive to long-term development, including respect for human rights.

After a decade of "adjustment", there are signs that basic needs is reemerging as a major issue in the development debate, at least as regards the poorest countries. The new emphasis results in part from a relearning of the basic lesson that a minimum level of social development must precede economic development, rather than emerging as a subsequent by-product. It is also more widely accepted that the success of policies aimed at improving the "pull-up" effects of the growth process depends on the "countervailing power" available to the poor.

The human element of basic needs/rights can be ensured only through the full participation of peoples/communities in decisions and actions affecting their lives. The local organisations which have been most successful in stimulating participation have generally been those whose members could expect some material benefit from their efforts. The struggle for basic needs/rights could provide one strong issue around which mobilisation could be successfully organised.

The achievement of basic rights would not be a mere palliative as it would eliminate some obstacles impeding authentic development and create new possibilities of moving towards the eventual achievement of such development. Thus the addressing of basic rights on a participative basis could be the initial step in a broader improvement and empowerment process.

Chapter 1

The Development Context

Introduction

This chapter sets the scene for the subsequent analysis of developments in relation to basic needs and human rights in the Third World. It examines the trends in overall economic development and poverty, and emphasises the divergences between different regions. Since external resources, especially aid, have been significant sources of financing for basic needs, the trends in these flows are also summarised and analysed. Thus the focus is more on outcomes than processes, and important underlying issues, including debt and trade, are not addressed here.

Country classifications

Although the term "developing country" is widely used it does not have a strict or consistent definition. In United Nations publications, the list of "developing countries and territories" is derived by a process of elimination, i.e. developing countries are those countries which are not either "developed market economy" or "socialist" (sub-divided into Eastern Europe and Asia). This is consistent with the broad division into First (developed), Second (socialist) and Third (developing) worlds. In effect, all the Asian socialist countries are relatively poor and would conventionally be classified as developing. Thus, over 80% of all countries are "developing" (broadly defined); they account for about 75% of the world's population, with China and India alone accounting for half of that (UNCTAD 1988).

The World Bank classifies countries solely on the basis of per capita GNP (Gross National Product). The group of "developing economies" is sub-divided into "low-income" (GNP per capita of $580 or less in 1989) and "middle-income" (GNP per capita between $580 and $6,000 in 1989). The range of incomes in the

15

low-income group is from $80 (Mozambique) to $480 (Sudan); the middle-income group ranges from $570 (Bolivia) to $5,420 (Libya). Spain and Ireland, with per capita incomes around $7,750 are at the bottom of the high-income group, with Switzerland at the top on over $27,500 (World Bank 1990). The figures do not include the non-members of the Bank – mainly countries in Eastern Europe – but most of the Asian socialist states are included.

There are some particular anachronisms in the different classifications. For example, high income countries such as Saudi Arabia, Singapore, Kuwait and the United Arab Emirates are regarded as developing countries by the United Nations. Hong Kong and Israel are not officially classified as developing but assistance to them is regarded as aid by the OECD. These countries all have per capita incomes higher than Ireland – twice as high in some cases.

Changes over time

In at least some middle-income developing countries, incomes are starting to approach the levels that "rich" countries enjoyed some thirty years ago. South Korea and Brazil, for example, are now at a level similar to that of Italy in 1960, while Colombia or Turkey would occupy a position similar to that then occupied by Ireland or Spain (ODI 1988). There is a blurred boundary between "developing" and "advanced" countries and a number of countries have graduated upwards over the years.

One way of marking this "graduation" is in terms of eligibility for different categories of World Bank loans – soft loans from the International Development Association (IDA) are only on offer to the poorest countries, while the harder (but still concessional) IBRD loans are open to middle income countries. Some 30 countries have graduated from IDA to IBRD loans since 1960; in Latin America, for example, only Guyana and Haiti are still eligible for soft loans. In addition to some European countries (including Ireland), Singapore and Venezuela have graduated beyond any World Bank lending.

At the other extreme, there is a clear group of countries at the bottom, mainly in Africa, where there has been little absolute progress and a persistent decline in income relative to the rest of the world. A separate sub-group of "least developed countries" (LLDCs) has been identified since 1979, on the basis of income per capita, adult literacy and share of the manufacturing sector in total output. There are now 42 countries in this category (compared to 31 at the beginning of the decade), with a combined population of 340 million, i.e. less than 10% of the total in the developing world. (For a list of the countries, see appendix to 1989 *World Development Report*). The per capita income of this group is only one-quarter that of the developing countries as a whole, the average daily calorie intake is 15% lower and infant mortality rates are 40% higher than the developing country average (UNCTAD 1989).

Thus the "Third World" is not a bloc in terms of income and wealth, but a very heterogeneous grouping of nations (ODI 1988). If there is little agreement about the boundary between the richer developing and the so-called developed countries, there is broad agreement on those at the bottom. Regardless of the precise method of measurement (whether through current prices and exchange rates or purchasing power parities), the poorest countries are largely the same now as in 1960. They include Ethiopia, Malawi, Mali, Tanzania and Zaire – Bangladesh has moved up a little while Ghana has moved down.

Over the last 20-30 years there has been neither the succession of economic take-offs which modernisation theory predicted, nor the continuously growing gap in income and welfare between the rich countries and the poor countries prophesied by some development theorists (Toye 1987). There have been some take-offs, mainly in East Asia, and some cases of retrogression, mainly in Africa. Thus the polarization that has taken place has done so within the Third World, but not between the Third World taken as a group and the developed economies.

Economic trends

From 1955 to 1980 world output tripled in real terms while population increased by over half: thus, income per head doubled, in both developed and developing countries (World Bank 1982). The structure of the world economy changed considerably over this period – for example, the share of world output produced by the United States fell from two-fifths to under one-quarter and Japan emerged as the second largest western economy. In the 1980s, economic performance varied widely between countries and continents, with faster growth in Asia and economic decline and regression in Africa and Latin America.

The diversity of experience is illustrated below for broad groups of countries for different time periods, i.e. before the first oil crisis (1965-73), the subsequent period (1973-80) and the

1980s. The indicator used is gross national product per capita, which captures both measured economic activity and population changes. The principal trends can be summarised as follows:
a) continuous improvement in East Asia (mainly China), as a result of high output growth and low population increase;
b) limited improvement in South Asia (including Bangladesh, India and Pakistan), where growth in output was moderate but population growth remained high;
c) poor overall performance in Africa, where the output record has been poor while population growth rates were high;
d) deteriorating performance in Latin America; and
e) declining average incomes in Africa and Latin America in the 1980s so that, for example, incomes in Africa are no higher now than they were a generation ago.

Table 1.1 Annual GNP per capita growth rates (%), 1965-89

Country Group	1965-73	1973-80	1980-89
High income economies	3.5	2.2	2.1
Low and middle income	3.5	2.4	2.7
Developing Regions			
Sub-Saharan Africa	3.0	0.1	-2.6
East Asia (incl China)	5.4	4.4	6.6
South Asia (incl India)	1.0	2.0	3.2
Latin America & Caribbean	4.1	2.4	-1.1
Europe/Mid. East/N.Africa	5.6	2.1	0.5

Source: Adapted from data in World Bank *World Development Report 1990*

There have been examples of rapid growth amongst many different types of economy, including those which have been tightly controlled with a large public sector (such as China), those where public and private decisions have been closely integrated (such as South Korea) and those with laissez-faire approaches (such as Hong Kong and Singapore). The faster growth of some countries is not easily explained but it is argued by some that the most important explanatory variables are political organisation and the administrative competence of government (Reynolds 1983).

Inequality and poverty

The relationship between inequality and development was long considered to be an inverted U, i.e. inequality increasing in the early stages of development and then later falling (Kuznets 1963). While this hypothesis is supported by the behaviour of the

18

$4300\,8478$

shares in income of the top 5%, the share of the bottom 20% appears to be around 5-6% for most income groups of countries (Stern 1989). Thus, increasing inequality in the course of economic development need not be synonymous with worsening impoverishment. The richest may get richer but the poorest may not get poorer.

Between 1960 and 1980 income inequality in the group of non-socialist developing countries increased substantially, especially in the low income countries and oil exporters, but decreased in the middle-income countries. Both within and inter-country inequalities increased but the greater disparities were those generated within countries (Adelman 1986). On the other hand, the amount of absolute poverty declined – the percentage of the population in non-socalist developing countries falling below the poverty level (in real purchasing power terms) declined by a third over the same period, from 47% to 30%.

The evidence suggests that there has been considerable progress in reducing the incidence of poverty but, with rapid population growth, a more modest reduction in the numbers of poor (World Bank 1990). For example, in India, which alone accounts for over one-third of the world's poor, their numbers actually increased between the early 1970s and early 1980s, although the percentage of the population below the poverty line fell from 54 to 43. There is a lack of reliable data for Sub-Saharan Africa, but it is estimated that the number of Africans in poverty increased by over 55 million between 1965 and 1985 (World Bank 1990). The average income shortfall, i.e. the extent to which the incomes of the poor fall short of the poverty line appears to have been reduced in most countries.

In the middle income countries, the share of the total income required to bring those below the poverty line up to it ("the poverty gap") is relatively small. For example, for Latin America, it was calculated at over 5% of GDP in 1970, falling to under 4% in 1980 and to around 2% by the year 2000 even on a low growth scenario (Prealc 1987). It would obviously be much larger for poorer countries – around 11 – 12% in India and Sub-Saharan Africa (World Bank 1990).

Financial resource flows

In the 1950s and early 1960s official aid was the principal mechanism through which capital flowed to the developing countries. Aid volumes stagnated in the 1960s but, as the international capital markets (especially the Eurodollar market) developed and more developing countries were judged credit-worthy, bank lending grew rapidly from the middle of the decade. There were further surges of bank lending in the early and mid 1970s and a boom in officially guaranteed export credits. Aid flows also increased greatly in real terms in the 1970s, thanks mainly to the OPEC donors. Following the emergence of the debt crisis in 1982, net bank lending fell rapidly and the recession in the developing countries cut back the demand for export credits.

The expectation that capital should move from developed countries to developing countries is grounded both in economic logic (i.e. higher rates of return in regions with under-used economic potential) and generally agreed policy objectives (OECD 1989). In the 1980s, however, the pattern and scale of capital flows shifted the other way and the United States became the world's largest importer of capital by far.

The principal figures for resource flows are summarised below for selected years. (Net resource flows include official and private grants, direct investment and long and short-term loans, minus loan repayments).

Table 1.2 Net resource flows to developing countries
($ billion, 1987 prices and exchange rates)

	1950-55	1960-61	1970	1980	1989
Total net	29	63	94	169	102
of which					
Aid* share	53%	56%	46%	32%	49%

Source: Adapted from Development Cooperation Reports (OECD)
* Official Development Assistance (ODA) plus NGO grants

The reduction of other flows and the repayment of debt, combined with an increase in aid in recent years, has meant that aid once again accounts for around half of all net resource flows to developing countries; NGOs account for about 4% of the total. (Aid accounts for almost two-thirds of the total for low-income countries and for over 90% in the case of the least developed group).

However, the above figures do not take account of interest and other investment income payments, which represent substantial outflows from at least some developing countries. The measure of "net financial transfers" (net resource flows minus interest and dividends) includes such flows. The figures for different regions during the 1980s are summarised below – they illustrate the

Bread and Freedom

diversity of experience and the dangers of aggregation. The outflows have mainly been from Latin America and the higher-income Asian countries, while there has been a continuing inflow into low-income Asia and Sub-Saharan Africa.

Table 1.3 Net financial transfers to developing countries ($ billion at 1987 prices and exchange rates)

	1980-82 Av.	1985	1989
Sub-Saharan Africa	16	13	14
N. Africa/Middle East	-11	- 6	- 6
Asian low-income	11	15	9
Other Asia	5	- 9	- 1
L. America/Caribbean	37	-31	-15
Other	8	- 1	1
Total Developing	**67**	**-17**	**3**
of which:			
Least Developed	14	1	13

Source: Development Cooperation Report (OECD 1990)

All the evidence points to continued low capital flows to the developing countries in the coming decade as official flows cannot fully offset the sharp reduction in private lending and investment (World Bank 1989). At the same time, it is recognised that they will require additional aid and other financial resources to cope with the challenges of the 1990s (OECD 1989).

Aid trends

Overall aid flows doubled in the 1950s, grew only slightly in the 1960s, increased by two-thirds in the 1970s and stagnated in the 1980s (all in real terms). There have been substantial changes in the sources of aid which have become more diverse. However, the member countries of the OECD Development Assistance Committee (DAC), i.e. most of the richer capitalist economies, have consistently provided the bulk of aid to developing countries. The contribution of the mainly Arab oil-producing countries increased rapidly in the 1970s but has since declined sharply. The socialist countries of Eastern European (designated as CMEA, i.e. Council for Mutual Economic Assistance), increased their aid flows in the 1980s – the USSR accounted for about 90% of their total.

The principal trends in official aid volumes are summarised below for the more recent years.

Table 1.4 Trends in official development assistance
($ billion, 1987 prices and exchange rates)

	1970-71	1975-76	1980-81	1988-89
World Total	31	44	52	51
of which:				
DAC Members	77%	63%	68%	87%
OPEC	5%	28%	23%	4%
CMEA	12%	7%	7%	8%
Other*	6%	2%	2%	1%

Source: Adapted from Development Cooperation Reports (OECD)
* Developing countries (e.g. China, India) & non-DAC OECD (Greece, Portugal, Spain)

In the 1950s, the United States provided at least half of all official aid – the remainder was accounted for by France and the United Kingdom, Australia, Canada, Japan and a number of European donors emerged in the 1960s so that the US share declined to less than a third. The OPEC donors emerged in the 1970s and the Nordic countries substantially increased their aid budgets. In the 1980s, the Japanese share increased markedly as the OPEC contribution declined; in 1989, Japan became the single largest aid donor in the world.

The trends in aid volumes for the major donors (which provide some 80% of all aid) are summarised below.

Table 1.5 Aid volumes (and % of GNP) for major donors
($ billion at 1987 prices and exchange rates)

	1970-71	1975-76	1980-81	1988-89
EEC Members*	11	13	17	22
	(0.42)	(0.45)	(0.39)	(0.50)
United States	8	8	8	8
	(0.31)	(0.26)	(0.27)	(0.18)
Japan	3	3	5	8
	(0.23)	(0.22)	(0.30)	(0.32)
Saudi Arabia	1	6	8	2
	(5.25)	(6.66)	(4.05)	(2.05
USSR	3	2	3	4
	(0.15)	(0.16)	(0.25)	(0.25)

Source: Adapted from Development Cooperation Reports (OECD)
* All 12 current EEC members, and including French aid to its overseas departments (DOM) and territories (TOM)

The only countries to meet the UN aid target of 0.7% of GNP in 1989 were Saudi Arabia (1.5%), Denmark (1.0%), Norway (1.0%), Sweden (1.0%), The Netherlands (0.9%), and France

(0.8% if aid to overseas departments and territories is included). The DAC average has fluctuated around half-way to the UN target (0.35%) for almost the last twenty years.

The Irish figure peaked at 0.28% in 1986 but has since fallen back to 0.17% – on the basis of OECD statistical conventions. On the other hand private aid (through voluntary agencies) is relatively much higher in Ireland than the average for the DAC countries – 0.08% of GNP versus 0.03%.

The combined official and NGO aid from Ireland is thus around 0.25% of GNP, compared to the current DAC average of 0.38%.

Aid recipients

Over the decade of the 1970s there was a substantial shift in the composition of total aid flows from DAC members away from aid based on donors' own interests and towards aid based on recipient need; this trend was reversed in the 1980s with shifts away from multilateral aid and within bilateral programmes (Maizels and Nissanke 1984).

In general, more aid does go to the poorer countries but there are some notable exceptions. In particular, the two largest developing countries, China and India, receive far less aid in relation to their GNPs than the norm for countries of their income level. On the other hand, countries which are of particular geopolitical significance to the larger donors get more aid, e.g. Egypt and Israel in the case of the United States. Over the past decade or so there has been a shift of emphasis from the Middle East to Africa, which now accounts for 35% of net aid receipts (compared to 20% in the mid-1970s). The Asian and Latin American shares have remained relatively constant, at around 33% and 13% respectively. There is no clear relationship between aid allocation and the basic needs records of recipient countries (Wood 1986).

The net receipts of official aid (ODA) from all sources in 1987-88 are shown below for the developing regions and selected countries. Many African countries and a small number in Asia and Latin America are highly aid-dependent, with net inflows equivalent to substantial shares of GNP and providing much of their foreign exchange. For Africa as a whole, aid provides half as much foreign exchange as do all export earnings but for countries like Ethiopia and Tanzania aid is of much greater relative importance.

(By comparison, the net budgetary inflow to Ireland from the European Community is equivalent to 5% of GNP and under 10% of export earnings).

Table 1.6 Net aid receipts as % of GNP and exports 1989

Region/Country	Per Capita Income (GNP)	Per Capita aid	% of GNP	% of Exports
Africa	$340	$28	8	43
of which:				
Ethiopia	$120	$14	12	167
Tanzania	$130	$39	32	353
Zambia	$390	$50	13	29
Asia	$448	$5	1	6
of which:				
Bangladesh	$180	$16	9	137
India	$340	$2	1	12
China	$350	$2	1	4
N. Africa/M. East	$2180	$11	1	3
of which:				
Egypt	$640	$31	5	61
Jordan	$1640	$72	6	30
Israel	$9790	$264	3	11
Latin America etc	$1950	$9	—	3
of which:				
Haiti	$360	$31	8	83
Bolivia	$620	$61	10	53
El Salvador	$1070	$87	8	73
All Developing	$800	$9	1	6

SOURCE: Adapted from OECD 1989 and WORLD BANK 1989

Bread and Freedom

Chapter 2

The Basic Needs Approach to Development

Historical background

In the 1950s and 1960s, industrialisation and the maximisation of economic growth were taken to be the mutually supportive objectives of development. Pursuit of these objectives met with considerable success and there was a marked acceleration in growth rates of national income and industrial output in a wide range of developing countries. For example, over the quarter century 1950-1975, average incomes (measured as Gross Domestic Product (GDP) per capita) increased by around 50% in India, 100% in the Philippines and 150% in Brazil (Morawetz 1977).

Trickle-down

The presumption was that economic growth would automatically "trickle down" to the poor or else governments would take collective action to promote their interests. (Some proponents of accelerated growth saw this as an activist strategy for impacting on poverty and thus preferred to call it the "pull-up" rather than the "trickle-down" approach, e.g. Bhagwati 1988).

Despite the primary emphasis on economic growth, social goals did feature strongly in some countries, for example China, Cuba and India. Similarly, the Charter of the Alliance for Progress, adopted by the Latin American countries and the United States in 1961, set numerical targets for reducing illiteracy and infant mortality, increasing school attendance and life expectancy, and extending access to potable water and sewage disposal (Martin 1985).

However, despite unprecedented rates of economic growth and impressive gains in health and literacy in the 1950s and 1960s, more people in developing countries were living in poverty at the end of the 1960s than a decade earlier. Capital-intensive and urban-oriented economic policies combined with the accelerating growth of population to expand the ranks of the poor. For example, in the early 1970s some 67% of the population in India, and 80% in Tanzania, had incomes below the poverty line (Chenery et al 1974). Population growth rates in the low and middle income countries were at historically unprecedented levels, of the order of 2.5% (and accelerating in many cases), compared to growth rates of around 0.5% in the present industrialised countries at a similar stage of development.

The benefits of economic growth clearly did not trickle down very far, partly because of the initial disadvantages of the poorer groups (e.g. in relation to access either to productive assets, such as land, or to essential social services such as health and education) and partly as a result of the relatively capital-intensive strategies adopted. There was also a general lack of political will or effective mechanisms (e.g. tax systems, social services) to ensure redistribution. The accumulating evidence of widespread immiserisation (resulting partly from rapid population growth) led to increased questioning of the development models and strategies being pursued; indeed the very concept of development came under intensive scrutiny.

Thus, one study of links between income distribution and a variety of economic, political and social variables for the 1950s and early 1960s concluded that "hundreds of millions of desperately poor people throughout the world have been hurt rather than helped by economic development" (Adelman and Morris 1973). This extreme view may not have been widely shared but it illustrates an important trend in informed analysis at the time.

Emergence of basic needs

In 1970 the UN General Assembly approved a strategy for the Second Development Decade which shifted from a dominant emphasis on growth in Gross National Product (GNP) to an effort to combine economic growth with greater satisfaction of "basic human needs", especially among the very poor. It advocated the reorientation of public policies and programmes to give priority to the generation of employment and to the delivery of basic educational, health, and nutrition services to the poor. Similarly, in 1973, the United States Congress amended the legislative mandate of the US Agency for International Development (USAID) to make the satisfaction of "basic human needs" the Agency's primary goal. It was argued by

26

commentators that development planners needed to be equally concerned, if not more so, with how the GNP increased as with the rate by which it increased (Grant 1973).

Employment promotion was initially viewed as the principal means of spreading the benefits of economic growth more evenly throughout the economy and the International Labour Organisation (ILO) organised employment missions to a large number of countries in the early 1970s. It soon became evident that unemployment as such was not the main problem, but rather low-productivity employment and poverty. The poor were mainly outside the organised sectors of the economy, i.e. peasant farmers in rural areas and members of the rapidly growing informal sector (or black economy) in urban areas. Thus the emphasis shifted to poverty-oriented development strategies designed to raise per capita incomes above a pre-determined poverty line, with the related aims of reducing income and social inequalities.

This policy of "redistribution with growth" (Chenery et al 1974) argued that economic growth was a necessary condition for eradicating poverty, but went on to recognise that it often entrenched and reinforced inequalities in the distribution of income, assets and power. It would obviously be politically difficult to redistribute existing assets but it was thought that the redistribution of increments of income would be easier – a proportion of the fruits of economic growth would be taxed and channelled into public services to raise the productivity of the poor. Remedial measures, including aid projects, were to be directed towards overcoming certain institutional handicaps which were thought to be responsible for keeping the incomes of the poor at low levels, e.g. lack of or insufficient access to productive assets, especially land and the right type of technology, and educational and health facilities. However, it became apparent that the results of such redistributions would be very modest, at any rate for low income countries, even if there was the political will to carry them out.

Enthronement of basic needs

The next major step on the international stage was the near unanimous adoption of a recommendation for a basic needs strategy by the World Employment Conference of the ILO in 1976 (ILO 1976). This was seen as the enthronement of basic needs in place of the discredited "King GNP" (Jolly 1976). In 1977, the member countries of the Development Assistance Committee of the OECD "reaffirmed their determination to direct, in cooperation with the developing countries, progressively larger efforts to programmes meeting basic human needs" (OECD 1978). The basic needs strategy also found strong support among international NGOs; for example, the Development Charter of the International Confederation of Free Trade Unions, adopted in 1978, asserted that "one of the main objectives of trade unions is to achieve the implementation of basic needs strategies" (Alston 1979).

Basic needs and the New International Economic Order

The establishment of a New International Economic Order (NIEO), as called for by the UN General Assembly in 1974, implies a reconstruction of the existing international system in the areas of trade, finance, and technology transfer as a means to improve development prospects and give developing countries more control over their own destinies.

Since the NIEO is concerned with international social justice, while basic needs is mainly concerned with domestic (intra-national) social justice, they should be complementary. Thus if reform of the international system generated more resources for developing countries, this could contribute to the satisfaction of basic needs. At the same time, the objective of meeting basic needs could help to mobilise international support, including increased aid flows. Thus the World Employment Conference, in putting forward this approach to development argued that "the satisfaction of basic needs is a national endeavour, but its success depends crucially upon the establishment of a New International Economic Order" (ILO 1976).

The NIEO by itself would be no guarantee that the governments of developing countries would use their increased resources to meet the needs of the poor. However, a basic needs programme which did not build on the self-reliance and self-help of countries and peoples would be in danger of degenerating into a global charity programme and could be counter-productive. At any rate, the two concepts soon became "grand designs on a collision course" (Galtung 1978).

Rejection at international level

At international meetings, delegates from the developing countries vehemently rejected the basic needs concept, for a number of reasons (Streeten et al 1981):

28

a) It was widely interpreted as a substitute for growth, modern-isation, industrialisation and self-reliance;
b) There was a fear that it would mean a diversion of aid to the poorest countries and perhaps even an overall reduction because of lack of absorptive capacity in the traditional basic needs sectors;
c) The introduction of basic needs criteria was seen to pave the way for donors to interfere in the autonomous setting of development priorities and, in particular, to introduce controversial political and social criteria of performance;
d) It was feared that it might be used as a thinly disguised protectionist device to keep down manufactured exports from developing countries;
e) Above all, it was strongly felt that the basic needs approach had been used as a diversionary tactic to draw attention away from the New International Economic Order.

Perhaps the strongest and most explicit criticism of the basic needs strategy was made by the Conference of Non-Aligned Foreign Ministers, meeting in Belgrade in 1978 (Alston 1979). They stated that "a basic needs approach at an international level would inevitably imply the imposition of global priorities on developing countries, thereby not only distorting the allocation of domestic resources of the latter but also perpetuating their technological dependence on the developed world".

Independent commentators have equally argued that the basic needs approach, while apparently radical in intent, was in fact backward-looking to a considerable extent (e.g. Dell 1979). In many formulations, there was a distinct lack of emphasis on the structural changes required to release the potential for development, while the role of modern industry and technology was played down. In order to meet the basic needs of the poor on a sustainable basis, it would be necessary to transform the productive structures and to increase industrial, as well as agricultural, output. A properly conceived basic needs strategy, which gave adequate attention to the production of basic goods and services, should, it was argued, positively aid industrialisation, e.g. by easing the demand constraint (Singh 1979).

Adoption at home

At the same time that developing countries were opposing the basic needs approach abroad, many of them (including Bangladesh, India, Kenya, Malaysia, Pakistan and the Philippines) were including basic needs objectives in their own national plans

(Hopkins and Van Der Hoeven 1983). For example, India indicated to the UN General Assembly in 1978 that it was "strongly against any attempt to direct the attention of the international community to alternative approaches to development cooperation, such as the basic needs approach". At the same time, the Indian Planning Commission adopted a Draft Five Year Plan for 1978-83, which listed three principal objectives, including action by the State to meet certain "basic needs" such as drinking water, literacy, elementary education, health care, rural roads, rural housing and minimum services in urban slums.

Conflict or excuse

There may be some underlying motivation for stressing the existence of a conflict between basic needs and the New International Economic Order (Stewart 1985). On the one hand, the industrialised countries have tended to use basic needs to avoid meeting the demands of the new order; on the other, some Third World leaders may wish to use such a conflict as a way of avoiding the required redistribution of public expenditure and of incomes. Thus, for both, the supposed conflict may be a useful political device.

Basic needs and adjustment

In the 1980s, most developing countries have suffered three types of external shocks: prices of their major export commodities have fallen; real interest rates have increased and international capital flows, particularly from commercial sources, have fallen (Selowsky 1987). The combination of increased debt service, reduced private investment and lending and relatively constant aid flows meant that the developing world paid out more to the industrial countries in the mid 1980s than it received from them.

The effect of these developments was to reduce disposable incomes (of individuals and governments) and to exacerbate the scarcity of foreign exchange. The latter in turn led to shortages of spare parts and other vital inputs, thus further restricting output and growth. The end result has been that, in some countries in Latin America, real income (GNP) per capita is less than it was a decade ago and, in some African countries, it is less than it was twenty years ago (World Bank 1989). The external shocks also served to expose internal weaknesses, whether in terms of economic and social structures or public policies.

Bread and Freedom

Adjustment

By the end of the 1970s, the basic needs approach was becoming dominant on the international scene, with support from bilateral aid donors and multilateral institutions, such as the ILO and the World Bank. However, the financial crisis that started in the 1970s and has dominated the development scene since then (together with shifts of political philosophy in some of the larger donor countries) led to a major switch in development policies.

The principal emphasis has shifted from growth to the "adjustment" of macroeconomic (mainly financial) imbalances, e.g. in the balance of payments and government budgets. In Asia the crisis has been less widespread but, for most countries in Africa and Latin America, adjustment policy has become "the dominating economic preoccupation for setting the frame and constraints within which all other economic and development issues have to be considered" (Cornia et al 1987).

While there is general agreement that developing countries have no alternative but to adapt to the changing world environment, the adjustment policies adopted have been severely criticised for their failure to promote growth and/or to protect the vulnerable. Underlying the standard approaches to adjustment programmes is the neoclassical economic argument that output, employment and prices are best determined by the free play of market forces. The inevitably deflationary character of most programmes has led to growing poverty through depressing employment and real incomes. In addition, there have been direct negative effects on some vulnerable groups as a result of rising urban food prices, cuts in food subsidies and reductions in social expenditure.

Adjustment with a Human Face

It must be recognised that deteriorations in living standards result from the overall economic situation, and not from adjustment policy as such. However, adjustment policies have generally disregarded the distributional and poverty implications of the measures introduced. In response to these developments, the concept of "Adjustment with a Human Face" (Cornia et al 1987) has been introduced to add a poverty alleviation dimension to adjustment, in much the same way as basic needs added such a dimension to growth. It may be thought of as "the basic needs approach to adjustment" (Cornia et al 1987).

As with basic needs, there is a strong and a weak version of "adjustment with a human face". The weak version tends to emphasise the short-term measures required to moderate what are seen as the transitional costs of policy changes. It is argued that adjustment operations help the poor over the long term, principally by establishing a more favourable policy environment that will promote growth and generate productive employment (World Bank 1987). The strong version, associated with UNICEF (Cornia et al 1987), involves a restructuring of the economy so that major imbalances are eliminated at a satisfactory level of output and investment while human capacities are maintained and developed. This is seen as "both a moral imperative and a practical pre-condition for sustained economic and social progress" (Grant 1989).

International environment

Since, for many countries, the adjustment problems of the 1980s arose from difficulties in the international environment, there is equally a need for adjustment in these international conditions, if national efforts are not to be undermined. This would require increased net financial flows through action on debt reduction, the stabilisation of commodity prices, a lowering of protectionist barriers and an increase in aid and investment.

Thus, as argued most cogently by UNICEF, "the derailment of the development effort in recent years now presents an opportunity to re-examine the direction of that effort and to make a new commitment to the kind of progress which meets the needs and enhances the capabilities of the poorest quarter of mankind" (UNICEF 1989).

Basic needs concepts

Basic needs is an approach to development, not a single strategy, in the sense that it gives priority to certain development objectives, but does not dictate the means by which these objectives are to be achieved (Stewart 1985). The main objective of the original basic needs approach was to satisfy the essential requirements of each country's population within one generation, or by the year 2000 (ILO 1976).

Two separate but complementary sets of targets were laid down: the first concerned mainly personal consumption needs such as food, shelter and clothing, while the second related to basic public services such as health, sanitation, the provision of safe drinking water, education, transport and cultural facilities. It was emphasised at the outset that the concept of basic needs was country-specific and dynamic; thus universal standards of minimum basic needs could not be defined.

Hierachy of needs

It is argued that there is not a single level of basic needs but a hierarchy (Streeten and Burki 1978). At the lowest level are those that have to be met for **basic survival**, e.g. minimal food and water. At the next level, are those that have to be met for **continued survival**, comprising a minimum of food and water, protection from fatal diseases and adequate shelter. At the third level, the satisfaction of basic needs covers **productive survival** and, in addition, protection from debilitating diseases, more food and some level of education. Finally, certain non-material needs must be added, like participation in making decisions affecting one's life and work and the relative component of poverty.

This classification is related to Maslow's hierarchy of human needs, beginning with the physiological (air, food and water) and moving to four levels of psychological needs – for safety, belongingness, esteem and self-actualisation (Maslow 1987). However, Maslow emphasised that attention to higher-level needs did not have to await the complete satisfaction of lower-level needs – "a more realistic description of the hierarchy would be in terms of decreasing percentages of satisfaction as we go up the hierarchy".

Because the lowest and most urgent needs are material, e.g. food, shelter, clothing etc., there is a danger that this could be generalised to a chiefly materialistic psychology. Maslow warns against forgetting that there are higher, non-material needs which are also basic (Maslow 1968). Beyond the simple physiological needs, there is no objective way of ranking other wants or needs: even people who are deprived of very basic physiological needs do consume non-basic goods and services (Stewart 1985).

Alternative approaches

Two distinctive features of the basic needs approach distinguish it from alternative approaches to development:

a) it focusses on actual consumption from a disaggregated, micro-level perspective; and

b) it gives primary attention to the role of public goods in national development (Weigel 1986).

The approach goes beyond abstractions such as GNP and supplements attention to how much is being produced, by attention to what is being produced, in what ways, for whom and with what impact (Hicks and Streeten 1979).

It is consistent with the entitlement approach, which was originally developed to deal with the question of famine (Sen

1981). Entitlements were defined as claims over food, which were made up of direct (subsistence) production, money incomes arising from the sale of goods and labour or other sources, and transfers from government or elsewhere. The set of entitlements could be extended to include all the basic needs bundle and minimum standards of fulfilment could be identified, although the appropriate cut-off point would not be objectively identifiable (Stewart 1985). It might be objected that basic needs are defined too much in terms of commodities, while the process of development is one of enhancing the capabilities of people, rather than simply expanding the supply of goods and services (Sen 1984).

It is difficult to fit the basic needs approach neatly into the main conventional schools of economic analysis, which do not discriminate between different types of goods. It represents an explicit departure from normal assumptions about consumer sovereignty, as it involves selecting certain types of goods for special attention. However, even the conventional economic approaches do permit exceptional treatment of public goods, which form a large part of basic needs, and are consistent with redistribution of income.

Interpretations and criticisms

While there is general agreement that a basic needs approach involves focussing on the fulfilment of certain minimum human needs, there is some confusion about the justification for selecting a particular bundle and this results in part from different interpretations of the approach (Stewart 1985).

Interpretations

The narrow view asserts that there are certain goods and services which every human being ought to have in order to live a decent life and that extra (or even exclusive) weight should be given to the achievement of this minimum package. In theory at least, this offers a well-defined set of targets for planning purposes; deficiencies can be measured and costs of meeting them estimated.

However, there are problems in justifying particular selections of items for inclusion and in determining priorities between them. In addition, most of the items are not wanted for themselves, but as means for improving the conditions of life. For example, numbers of doctors or nurses are not ends in themselves but rather means for delivering health care/education which contribute to improved health.

The second view defines the objective more broadly, as being the improvement of the conditions of life, i.e. "the full-life objective" (Stewart 1985). A minimal definition confines the objective to health and perhaps education, while a broader one would include the conditions necessary for the enjoyment of culture, for full participation in the political process and so on. The bundle of goods to be included is selected according to the effects they have on the full-life objective. This may lead to a different bundle from those chosen with respect to the first view. For example, the bundle of goods approach almost invariably selects access to clean water as one essential input but, while access is important, quality matters much less as people can and do convert dirty water into clean and vice versa.

Ideological views

These distinctions are paralleled by differing ideological views. Mainstream commentators regard basic needs as a complementary strategy to the traditional emphasis on economic growth, in effect another version of "redistribution with growth" (Friedmann 1979). Thus basic needs would allow trickle down to work for the majority while getting on with the task of raising the standard of living of those whom the market threatened to bypass completely. It is seen as supplementing market tendencies and various governmental policies that favoured greater equality, but not substituting for them (Fishlow 1984).

On the other hand, radicals argue that it is the growth strategy itself which is responsible for much of the poverty which basic needs approaches are intended to correct. The latter would emphasise the production changes which are required to ensure the supply of basic goods and services and the creation of employment on a large scale.

According to one interpretation, the basic needs approach is revolutionary because it calls for radical redistribution, not only of income and assets, but also of power, and for the political mobilisation of the poor themselves. At the other extreme, the approach has been interpreted as a minimum welfare package to keep the poor quiet and to prevent the radical reforms required to bring about more egalitarian development.

An intermediate interpretation is that basic needs have been met by a variety of political regimes and that a revolution is neither a necessary nor a sufficient condition. Thus a major study concluded that "improvements in Basic Needs performance do not require extreme achievements with respect to income distribution, nor with respect to economic growth; they are potentially within the reach of most types of economy" (Stewart 1985).

The differing interpretations were summarised in the foreword to the World Bank publication on basic needs as follows:

"To some, the concept of providing for the basic needs of the poorest represents a futile attempt to redistribute income and provide welfare services to the poor, without stimulating corresponding increases in their productivity to pay for them. To others, it conjures up the image of a move towards socialism, and whispered references are made to the experience of Cuba and China. Yet still others see it as a capitalist conspiracy to deny industrialization and modernization to the developing countries and thereby to keep them dependent on the developed world. It is amazing how two such innocent, five-letter words could mean so many different things to so many different people" (Mahbub ul Haq in Streeten et al 1981).

Operational implications

It is hardly surprising that differing interpretations of what is meant by a basic needs strategy have, in turn, given rise to different favoured approaches, which are discussed below.

Direct delivery

One method of implementation consists of counting the number of the deprived, estimating the costs of goods and services needed to eradicate deprivation and delivering them to the target group – this has been called the "count, cost and deliver" approach (Streeten et al 1981). Thus it was estimated in the late 1970s that up to 800 million people were suffering shortfalls in core basic needs, identified as food, clothing, safe drinking water and shelter. In order to meet these shortfalls by the year 2000, the resource requirements were estimated at $30 – 40 billion per annum (Streeten and Burki 1978). If Western aid donors (OECD members) were to concentrate their efforts on the poorest countries and contribute half of the costs involved, total aid flows would have to double (Streeten et al 1981). Quite apart from basic questions of desirability (e.g. lack of participation by recipients) and feasibility, such a direct delivery approach would be expensive, unsustainable and ultimately ineffective unless supported by a range of other actions.

Growth and earnings

Another approach insists on the need to provide earnings opportunities for the poor, to raise their productivity and to improve their access to both inputs and markets. The background document for the World Employment Conference in 1976 estimated that extremely high growth rates, averaging 10 – 13 % p.a, would be required to meet specified minimum needs in the Third World by the year 2000. With redistribution, the required growth rates would be two or three points lower but still much higher even than those experienced in the boom years of the 1960s.

There are also shortcomings in the income-orientation approach as regards access to basic needs. For example, some basic needs can be satisfied more effectively through public services (e.g. education, health), through subsidised goods and services, or through transfer payments. There is also some evidence that consumers are not always efficient, especially in optimising nutrition and health, and there is often maldistribution within households, to the detriment of the needs of women and children (Streeten et al 1981).

Participation

Another interpretation stresses the need to mobilise the social and political power of the poor and to ensure full participation in the design, execution and monitoring of anti-poverty projects. Participation is seen as both an end in itself and as a means of satisfying material needs (Lisk 1985). Thus the International Development Strategy adopted by the UN General Assembly in 1980 states that "the ultimate aim of development is the constant improvement of the well-being of the entire population on the basis of its full participation in the process of development and a fair distribution of the benefits therefrom".

The ILO Director, in his report to the World Employment Conference (ILO 1976), had argued that: "A basic needs oriented policy implies the participation of the people in making the decisions which affect them... The satisfaction of an absolute level of basic needs as so defined should be placed within a broader framework – namely the fulfilment of basic human rights, which are not only ends in themselves but also contribute to the attainment of other goals". However, the resolutions of the Conference did not refer to this broader human rights framework.

Chapter 3

Trends in the Provision of Basic Needs

Definition and measurement

There are three factors to be taken into account when defining basic needs, namely the components (e.g. education, food etc), the indicators of progress (e.g. calorie intake) and the targets or levels of the indicators at which the needs are satisfied (e.g. x calories per capita).

Although there is much disagreement about precisely how to define basic needs, there is general agreement about a core which includes food, water, health, education and shelter. For example, the ILO argued that basic needs included "certain minimum requirements of a family for private consumption: adequate food, shelter and clothing, as well as certain household equipment and furniture...[and] essential services provided by and for the community at large, such as safe drinking water, sanitation, public transport and health, educational and cultural facilities" (ILO 1976)

However, meeting these core needs is seen only as a first step in meeting the total human needs of people. Non-material aspects, such as security and participation in cultural life and political activity, are clearly important components of the desired full-life objective but are very difficult to define and measure. There are also many complementarities, so that achievement in non-material areas, e.g. participation, both depends on and itself partly determines achievements on the basic material rights (Stewart 1988).

Many of the so-called basic needs are inputs rather than ultimate goals; thus nutrition, water supply and sanitation are valued because they improve the health status of the population. In order to measure basic needs performance, it would be desirable to select output indicators (e.g. life expectancy) as far as possible, rather than input indicators (e.g. numbers of doctors). On the other hand, input measures are useful indicators of the resources committed and may reflect government commitment and efforts to provide public services (Hicks and Streeten 1979).

Another general rule would be to try as much as possible to choose indicators which measure distributional aspects, e.g. the percentage of the population above certain target levels (Hopkins and Van Der Hoeven 1983). National averages, such as calories per capita, can conceal maldistribution both between and within households. This is a lesser problem for measures such as life expectancy, where an upper limit is determined by physiological factors and the range of variation is thus narrowed. Literacy figures are not subject to the same problem of distribution since they measure the proportion of the adult population who are literate.

In practice, the choice of indicators is determined to a large extent by the availability of statistics. While there is a wealth of reasonably reliable data on inputs, into education and health systems for example, there is a scarcity of accurate output measures. Thus, changes over time or between countries can be due to methods of measurement as much as any actual differences. Of greater concern must be the paucity of micro-level data relating to the distribution of basic needs inputs and achievements, e.g. by area, gender and income level.

Composite indices

In the same way that GNP and related measures provide consistent measures of output, attempts have been made to devise summary measures or indicators of welfare. Efforts to find such a composite index have foundered on a variety of difficulties, e.g. how to determine an adequate measure of welfare, how to quantify the components, how to establish international comparability and so on (Morris 1979). Thus, an OECD working party on social indicators concluded that a single unitary "social well-being" index serving the same summarisation purpose as GNP should be ruled out as giving almost no information whatsoever (OECD 1976).

Physical Quality of Life Index

A less ambitious attempt was made to devise a Physical Quality of Life Index (PQLI) which could serve as a creative complement to

40

GNP (Morris 1979). The prime objective was to measure the performance of the world's poorest countries in meeting the most basic needs of people; thus the index was concerned only with the results achieved and not with the methods.

In selecting appropriate components from the myriad of possible indicators, ethnocentric measures of political or economic development, including health and nutrition standards (e.g. medical facilities and staffing, estimated calorie requirements), were excluded. Indicators were included which: a) measured results not inputs, b) reflected distribution, c) were based on data which were relatively easy to collect and process, and d) lent themselves to international comparison. Only three indicators were considered to meet all of these criteria – infant mortality, life expectancy (at age one) and basic literacy.

A simple indexing system was adopted, using a scale of 0 to 100 for each indicator, where 0 represented an explicitly defined "worst" performance and 100 represented an explicit "best" performance. The ranges were based on an examination of historical experience, modified where appropriate by expectations of possible change. Thus, for infant mortality, the range was 229 to 7 deaths per thousand births; for life expectancy the range was from 38 to 77 years, and for literacy it was 0 to 100. The scores for each of these indicators were then averaged to give the Physical Quality of Life Index (PQLI) for each country, on the scale of 0 to 100. Thus, in the early 1970s, Sweden had the highest PQLI value (97) and Guinea-Bissau the lowest (12); other values included Ireland (93), China (69), India (43) and Ethiopia (20) (Morris 1979). In India, for example, the overall index had gone from 14 in 1949 to 40 in 1970, but the average level concealed substantial gender differences – a PQLI of 45 for males but only 35 for females.

The principal weakness of the PQLI is that there is no particular reason for giving equal weight to the three indicators which it combines. If, for a given country, the scores for each indicator are very close then it would seem simpler and sounder to select one of them to stand as the overall indicator of social development. On the other hand, if the scores are markedly different then the PQLI makes a concealed value judgement, by giving each indicator an equal weighting (UNICEF 1989).

In practice, the PQLI has not gained wide acceptability. Most analysts have instead adopted single indicators of basic needs achievement, e.g. life expectancy (Hicks 1982) or infant mortality (Goldstein 1985). Governments and various international organisations select their indicators according to their own priorities – UNICEF, for example, favours the under-five mortality rate (U5MR), supplemented by the illiteracy rate.

Human Development Index

The United Nations Development Programme (UNDP) has undertaken to produce an annual report on the human dimension of development. The first such report (UNDP 1990) introduced a new Human Development Index, based on three indicators – life expectancy, adult literacy and income per head. [The latter is not derived from the conventional GNP figures, but from purchasing-power-adjusted GDP estimates].

In order to construct the composite index, minimum and desirable values were specified for each of the indicators. The minimum values were chosen by taking the lowest national value recorded for each indicator in 1987, e.g. a life expectancy of 42 in Afghanistan, an adult literacy rate of 12% in Somalia. The desirable values were Japan's life expectancy of 78 years in 1987, an adult literacy rate of 100% and the average of the official "poverty lines" in nine industrial countries, adjusted for purchasing power. The level of a country's deprivation was measured for each indicator and the three were averaged to give a deprivation index, which was subtracted from 1 to derive the human development index.

The index was calculated for 162 countries, with Japan at the top and Djibouti at the bottom. Ireland ranked joint 18th, on a par with Austria and the USA. Countries such as Chile, Costa Rica, Jamaica, Sri Lanka, Tanzania and Thailand did much better on their human development ranking than on their income ranking, while oil and mineral exporting countries, in particular, did much worse.

The Human Development Index is open to some of the same criticisms as the Physical Quality of Life Index, i.e. for combining disparate items, giving equal weight to the three indicators and for incorporating average figures which ignore distribution. An additional criticism concerned the selection of the target level of income, thus implicitly viewing development as a discrete state to be attained, rather than a progression (Nolan 1990). Although modifications have been made to the Index (UNDP 1991) it remains to be seen if it gains any wider acceptance than the PQLI.

Overall trends on basic needs

The three most commonly used single indicators are:
1) life expectancy at birth,

2) adult literacy and
3) the mortality rate of children under 5 years.
Life expectancy is the simplest measure of achievement with respect to health and is obviously influenced by a range of basic needs goods and services, including nutrition, and security. Literacy is not only a broad measure of achievement in education (formal and non-formal) but also represents an increased potential for participation in political and development activities.

The under-5 mortality rate (U5MR) reflects the combined effect of many factors, including the nutritional health and the health knowledge of mothers, the availability of maternal and child health services, the income and food position of the family, the access to clean water and sanitation and the overall safety of the child's environment (UNICEF 1989).

Life expectancy

The trends in life expectancy since 1950 are summarised below for different country groups.

Table 3.1 Life expectancy (years) 1950-89

	1950	1960	1970	1980	1989
All developing	43	48	54	58	63
Low income	41	47	53	57	62
Africa	35	39	43	46	51
China	–	41	52	64	70
India	–	42	47	52	59
Middle income	46	50	55	60	66
Oil exporters	–	46	51	57	58
Industrial (OECD)	68	70	71	74	76

Source: *World Development Reports* (World Bank)

Thus, for developing countries as a whole and for the major sub-groups, the average life expectancy has increased by almost half since 1950 and there is no indication of any slow-down in progress. In this respect they have achieved as much improvement over about thirty years as required two centuries for the currently industrialised countries, which only attained similar levels in the 1930s. As a result, population growth in the developing world is at least four times the rate of increase recorded in the industrialised countries at the time of their own industrial revolutions.

There are still wide variations in life expectancy between

regions and countries, with Africa lagging behind. The values range from a low of 42 years in Sierra Leone to a high of around 70 in Sri Lanka and a number of Latin American and Caribbean countries. On this indicator at least, the rate of progress has been similar for females and males. Of particular interest is the much better performance of China (70 years) than India (59).

Literacy

The trends in the adult (over 15 years of age) literacy rate since 1950 are summarised below. The figures for China have been excluded from the relevant averages, as they are only available for the later years.

Table 3.2 Literacy rate %: 1950-85

	1950	1960	1970	1980	1985
All developing*	33	38	46	52	60
Low income*	20	27	29	38	46
Africa	–	17	17	29	48
China	–	–	–	66	69
India	–	28	33	36	43
Middle income	48	49	64	68	75
Oil exporters	–	14	26	32	53
Industrial (OECD)	95	97	98	99	99

Source: *World Development Reports* (World Bank) * Excluding China

Considerable progress has been made here also so that almost 60 per cent of adults in the developing world (including China) are now literate, by comparison with around one-third in 1950. Africa has only recently started to make significant advances and in a number of countries (e.g. Mali and Somalia) over 80 per cent of the population is still illiterate. In this respect also, India lags far behind China. In many low income countries, in particular, the literacy rate among men is at least twice that among women. [The most extreme case is Afghanistan, where the differential is 5:1, i.e. a literacy rate of only 8 per cent of women, compared to 39 per cent of men (UNICEF 1989)].

Under 5 mortality

The under-5 mortality rate (U5MR) is the number of children who die before the age of five for every 1,000 live births. The trends since 1950 are summarised below; the rate of progress is measured by the average annual reduction rate (see UNICEF 1989).

44

Table 3.3 Under-5 mortality and reduction rates: 1950-87

	U-5 mortality rates			Reduction rates (%pa)	
	1950	1980	1987	1950-80	1980-87
All developing	295	138	120	2.5	2.0
Africa (All)	332	191	172	1.8	1.5
Asia (South)	344	200	158	1.8	3.3
Asia (East)	273	51	45	5.4	1.8
Asia (Other)	279	112	102	3.1	2.4
C & S America	201	91	79	2.6	2.0
Industrialised	84	20	18	4.7	1.5

Source: *State of the World's Children 1989* (UNICEF)

For the developing world, excluding China, the under-5 mortality rate has been more than halved since 1950. In China, which accounted for almost 30 per cent of such mortalities in 1950, the rate has been brought down from 280 to 40 (a level only reached in Ireland in the 1950s). Substantial progress has been made in all regions but more slowly in Africa and South Asia (including India). As a result, although the total number of births in the developing countries has increased by half since 1950, the number of under-5 mortalities has fallen by well over one-third; some 70 per cent of the reduction is due to the progress in China alone.

As might be anticipated, there has been little reduction in mortality rates in those countries experiencing civil wars and/or droughts; thus in Cambodia the rate (199) is almost double that of neighbouring countries. In Africa, mortality rates are high in countries such as Angola and Mozambique (around 290) and Ethiopia (226), but are equally high in countries not facing similar problems, e.g. Malawi and Sierra Leone (around 260).

The overall rate of improvement is slowing down as the earlier figures were heavily influenced by the dramatic progress achieved in China. For the developing countries as a whole, the under-5 mortality rate declined by 2.8% per year on average between 1950-55 and 1960-65; by 2.6% per year in the following decade and by 2.0% between 1970-75 and 1980-85 (United Nations 1988). The latter rate of decline continued into the 1980s.

Some key sectors

Developments in relation to some of the key instruments or inputs which might be expected to have contributed to the above results are summarised below.

Food and nutrition

In most regions of the developing world, with the notable exception of Sub-Saharan Africa, food production has outpaced population growth over the past quarter-century. As a result of this increased domestic production and rising imports, food availability (calories per capita per day) has significantly improved for a large number of countries.

The most spectacular gain was in China, where there has been a 50 per cent increase in calorie supply per capita, but from a very low base. In drought-affected Africa, on the other hand, food supplies at one stage in the early 1980s fell back to the levels of twenty years previously and have only recovered slightly since then.

Trends in the average level of food availability since the early 1960s are summarised below; three-year averages are used in most cases because of large annual fluctuations.

Table 3.4 Food availability (calories per day), 1962-88

	1961-63	1969-71	1979-81	1986-88
Developing countries	1957	2113	2321	2319
Sub-Saharan Africa	2050	2100	2150	2097
Asia (excl China)	1970	2070	2200	2340
China	1713	1976	2289	2637
Latin America	2380	2520	2680	2732
Near East/N.Africa	2220	2370	2850	2695
Developed countries	3090	3260	3370	3333

Source: FAO (1987) and FAO (1990)

The average figures presented above conceal the highly unequal distribution of food, both between and within households. Of particular concern is the incidence of under-nutrition but there is no consistent set of figures on individual food intake relative to need. The Food and Agriculture Organisation (FAO) of the United Nations takes the household as the unit of measurement, while the World Bank takes the broader category of the income group (Naiken 1988).

According to international standards, persons are defined as undernourished if their calorie intake is below 1.2-1.4 (depending on assumptions) times the Basal Metabolic Rate. The higher limit is adopted here to account for intra-household variations – it is equivalent to around 1600-1700 calories per day, depending on the country.

46   *Bread and Freedom*

In its World Food Surveys, FAO has estimated the level of undernutrition in developing countries for different points in time, from the late 1960s to the early 1980s (FAO 1985), but these figures exclude China and other centrally planned economies in Asia. In most cases, there has been a decline in the proportion of the population undernourished but a rise in the absolute numbers. The figures are summarised in the table below.

Table 3.5 Undernutrition: persons (mn) and % of population

	1969-71		1979-81		1983-85	
Sub-Saharan Africa	86	(33%)	110	(31%)	142	(35%)
Near East/N.Africa	41	(23%)	25	(11%)	24	(9%)
Asia	281	(29%)	288	(24%)	291	(22%)
Latin America	51	(19%)	52	(15%)	55	(14%)
Total	460	(27%)	475	(22%)	512	(22%)

Source: FAO (1985)

Although the position in Africa should have improved somewhat after the drought years of the early 1980s, the trend is still one of increasing numbers of undernourished people. In Asia (excluding China) and Latin America, the increased food availability has led to a reduction in the proportion of people undernourished but a continuing (if slow) increase in their number.

Similar figures are not available for China but per capita nutrient availability only returned to its 1958 (pre-famine) level in the mid-1970s. By 1980, when national food availability was well above requirements, 10-15% of China's population of 964 million people still lived in provinces where average nutrient availability fell below 90% of requirements (Croll 1986).

High mortality resulting from regular deprivation exceeds by a large margin the mortality resulting from famine and other disasters, although the latter are more dramatic. It is estimated that the extra famine deaths in China in 1958-61 (29.5 million people) would have been exceeded in India in less than 9 years because of its continuing higher "normal" mortality (Sen 1987). Thus, despite the massive scale of the Chinese famine, India still has a substantially worse record in relation to avoidable deaths.

In summary, over 500 million people in the developing countries do not have enough to eat on a regular basis. A World Bank study similarly concluded that approximately 500 million people consumed less than 90% of the recommended number of calories (Reutlinger and Alderman 1980). The results of this malnutrition can be seen particularly in the children, where it leads to stunting and wasting.

UNICEF has estimated that 25-30% of children under-5 in the lower income countries (excluding China) suffered mild-moderate malnutrition over the period 1980-86, and at least 5% suffered severe malnutrition. The prevalence of wasting was estimated at around 10% in children of 12-23 months, while over 40% of those aged 24-59 months showed evidence of stunting. Although based on highly incomplete data (see UNICEF 1989), these stark figures serve to emphasise the impact of malnutrition on the most vulnerable.

Health

The achievements in this sector were presented above, in terms of improvements in life expectancy and reductions in infant and childhood mortality. Other health indicators relate to inputs rather than results, e.g. numbers of health personnel, government expenditure levels etc.

The staffing position is usually expressed in terms of the number of people per health worker, physician or nurse. The trends over the past twenty years are summarised below – comprehensive figures are only available up to 1984.

Table 3.6 Population per physician/nursing person 1965-84

| | No. per physician | | No. per nurse | |
	1965	1984	1965	1984
All developing	8,270	4,790	5,020	1,900
Low income	9,760	5,580	6,010	2,200
Africa	33,200	23,850	5,420	2,460
China	1,600	1,000	3,000	1,710
India	4,880	2,520	6,500	1,700
Middle income	4,060	2,520	2,190	980
Industrial (OECD)	870	450	420	130

Source: *World Development Report 1990* (World Bank)

The number of physicians has risen almost twice as fast as the population and the number of nursing staff almost three times as fast in most of the developing world. However, the staffing levels are still highly inadequate in many countries in Africa, e.g. only one doctor for 79,000 people in Ethiopia. In general, the industrialised countries have 11-15 times as many health

48   *Bread and Freedom*

personnel relative to population as the low income countries.

In addition, health facilities and staff are often very unevenly distributed, to the detriment of rural areas. Thus, while most people in urban areas have at least physical access to health services, only a minority of rural dwellers have such access in many countries, e.g. under 20% in Afghanistan, Myanmar, Ivory Coast, Peru and Zaire (UNICEF 1989). Similarly, there are wide variations in the proportion of births attended by trained personnel and these are broadly correlated with the maternal mortality rates (per 100,000 live births), as illustrated below for groups of countries classified by under-5 mortality levels.

Table 3.7 Attended births and maternal mortality, 1980s

Under-5 Mortality	% of births attended by trained personnel	Maternal mortality
Over 170	23%	420
95-170	51%	140
31-94	74%	91
Under 30	99%	11

Source: UNICEF (1989)

Even where staff and facilities are present, government funds for drugs and other requirements are often inadequate, partly because of limited resources and partly because of inadequate commitment. Across a wide range of low and middle income countries, only about 5% of central government expenditure is allocated to health, while twice as much is spent on defence (UNICEF 1989). The combination of low incomes and often low priority resulted in 1988 in government health expenditure per head of $1-2 in the low-income countries, compared to over $600 per head in the industrialised countries.

Education

It is easy to measure participation in this sector, e.g. by enrolment rates at different levels, but more difficult to measure impact on a consistent basis.

The following table summarises the trends in enrolment over the past twenty years, expressed as the ratio of pupils to the population of school-age children. Gross enrolment ratios may exceed 100% because many pupils may be younger or older than the country's standard school age, e.g. 6-11 years at primary level.

Table 3.8 Education enrolment (% of age group), 1965-87

	Primary		Secondary		Tertiary	
	1965	1988	1965	1988	1965	1988
All developing	78	105	22	42	3	8
Low income	73	105	20	37	2	3
Africa	41	67	4	18	0	2
China	89	134	24	44	1	2
India	74	99	27	41	5	9
Middle Income	92	104	26	55	6	17
Industrial (OECD)	104	103	63	95	21	41

Source: *World Development Report 1991* (World Bank)

Primary education is becoming almost universal in most of the developing countries but gender differences persist, e.g. over 75% of boys but only 57% of girls attend primary school in Africa (World Bank 1990). There have been improvements in persistence of school attendance also; thus almost 80% of those entering primary school in 1984 persisted to grade 4, compared to just over 60% of the 1970 cohort. UNESCO assumes permanent literacy may be achieved by the fifth grade (World Bank 1980).

The proportion of the relevant age group attending secondary school has almost trebled in developing countries since 1960, from 14% to 42%, but there are still only 75 females per 100 males at this level. Despite significant advances, the lowest enrolments are to be found in Africa, e.g. only 4% in Tanzania compared to 18% in Bangladesh. Although the most rapid expansion has been at the tertiary level, this is where the widest gap is to be found between the developed and the developing worlds, i.e. five times as high a proportion of the relevant age group attend third-level colleges in the richer countries.

The governments of most developing countries have always given priority to education and have allocated a relatively high share of their resources to the sector. Thus, low income countries (excluding China and India) allocated an average of 9% of central government expenditure to education in 1989, i.e. over three times that allocated to health (World Bank 1990). (Ireland, like most developed countries, allocates a slightly higher proportion to health than to education).

Water, sanitation and shelter

Considerable progress has been made since 1970 in providing safe water and, to a lesser extent, adequate sanitation. The

Bread and Freedom

percentages of people in rural and urban areas of developing countries with access to such facilities are shown below. (China is excluded as data are not available on a comparable basis).

Table 3.9 Access to safe water and sanitation, 1970-90 (percentages of people)

	Safe water supply			Adequate sanitation		
	1970	1980	1990	1970	1980	1990
Urban areas	66	75	82	30	54	72
Rural areas	13	32	63	12	14	49

Source: UNICEF 1989, 1991

These averages conceal wide variations between countries. In Sub-Saharan Africa, for example, the proportion of the rural population with access to safe water varies from only 7% in Sierra Leone, through 21% in Kenya and 42% in Tanzania, to 48% in Rwanda.

It is difficult to compile comparable figures on shelter, but it is agreed that a high proportion of both rural and urban people live in highly inadequate accommodation, which contributes to health and other problems. In Latin America, for example, it is estimated that no less than half of the rural and one-third of the urban housing stock should be either rebuilt or substantially improved, at a cost equivalent to over 3% of the region's GDP (Prealc 1987).

Security

Although difficult to measure in all its aspects, a number of indicators would suggest that insecurity is increasing in the developing countries.

For example, the number of "natural" disasters appears to be increasing. Thus the Red Cross and Red Crescent societies recorded an average of 81 disasters per year in the 1970s, compared to 54 in the 1960s and the numbers affected increased from an annual average of 28 million people to 48 million over the same period. Droughts and floods accounted for about 90% of all recorded disasters. Although natural forces triggered the disaster events, important contributory causes were human vulnerability resulting from poverty, serious environmental degradation and rapid population growth (Wijkman and Timberlake 1984).

Similarly, the frequency of wars has increased and, with one exception, all the major wars since 1945 have been in the Third World – albeit with varying degrees of superpower involvement. Thus, in the 1950s the average was 9 wars per year, in the 1960s it was 11 and, in the 1970s and early 1980s, it was 14 per year (Sivard 1983). It is estimated that the number of deaths resulting from wars over the period 1945-1983 exceeded 16 million (including some ten million civilians), but that 15 million people died each year over the same period from social neglect (as measured by the gap between actual life spans in different countries and the highest national averages – Sivard 1983).

One of the most unfortunate consequences of the natural disasters and wars has been the increasing numbers of refugees, which practically doubled during the 1980s. There are now an estimated 15 million refugees or displaced people in the world, 10 million in Asia and 4 million in Africa.

Indicators of civil and political rights

In addition to material poverty, there is "political poverty" in many developing and industrialised countries. This has been defined as "the unequal distribution of opportunities and mechanisms for intervention in the decisions which affect development processes for the society as a whole" (Prealc 1987). A number of complications arise in trying to compare perform-ance between countries and over time in relation to civil and political rights. Many of the specific measures are ethnocentric and analysts tend to extrapolate from their own, usually Western, experience. In order to summarise and, to a limited extent, quan-tify developments, indices of performance have been prepared.

The table below summarises selected country scores in relation to both civil and political rights on one of the better-known indices (Taylor and Jodice 1983). Countries are scored from 1 to 7, with higher scores indicating poorer performance. Countries which are more concerned with equality than individualism do not score well on these indices, because the authors are concerned with "justice based upon autonomy for groups and individuals" and with "the balancing of the political rights of majorities against the civil liberties of minorities".

Although such indices must be treated with caution, the broad picture which they paint of the deprivation of civil and political rights in the Third World is confirmed by other sources. For example, three-quarters of developing countries are reported to have used violence against the public, e.g. in the form of torture, "disappearances" and summary executions (Sivard 1983). Over half of the developing countries are under some form of military rule, by comparison with one-quarter in 1960 (Sivard 1987). The association between institutionalised violence and military controlled governments is particularly strong.

Table 3.10 Indices of rights in selected countries, 1970s

Political Rights Index Country	Score	Civil Rights Index Country	Score
Ireland	1.0	Costa Rica	1.0
Sri Lanka	2.0	Ireland	1.6
Malaysia	2.7	Sri Lanka	3.0
Pakistan	4.3	Nigeria	4.0
Zambia	5.0	Indonesia	5.0
Tanzania	6.0	Tanzania	6.0
China	6.7	China	6.7
Uganda	7.0	Uganda	7.0

Source: Taylor and Jodice (1983)

Recent trends in basic needs provision

After decades of steady progress on basic needs, there has been noticeable deterioration in some areas in the 1980s as the combined effects of recession, financial outflows, declining commodity prices and adjustment programmes have reduced the resources available to households and governments in the developing world. Throughout most of Africa and much of Latin America, average incomes have fallen by 10% to 20% over the last decade. On the other hand, average incomes and living standards have continued to improve in the Asian countries which contain the majority of the world's absolute poor (e.g. China, India and Pakistan).

Slowdown in progress

Despite the serious economic problems experienced, the principal basic needs indicators analysed above still registered progress for all regions during this decade. Thus life expectancy (Table 3.1) and adult literacy rates (Table 3.2) continued to improve, while under-5 mortality rates (Table 3.3) declined steadily. However, the rate of reduction in under-five mortality has slowed down in many countries, even excluding those affected by war or civil strife. It has been estimated that, in 16 such countries (10 in Africa and 6 in Latin America), the number of child deaths per year is around 650,000 more than would have been the case if the 1970-80 rate of decline had continued (UNICEF 1989).

Public expenditure

The combined effects of recession, debt (interest and capital) repayment and adjustment programmes have forced many governments to cut back on expenditure, including that on social sectors. For example, in Sub-Saharan Africa real government expenditure per capita (excluding interest payments) fell by one-third between 1980 and 1985, leading to a cut of one quarter in social spending per head (World Bank 1990). Over the same period, the average cut in social spending per capita in Latin America was 18%, but varied considerably between countries, e.g. falling by 30% in Costa Rica but rising by a similar proportion in Chile (Pfeffermann 1987).

In Africa, public expenditure on education has stagnated during the 1980s (UNECA 1988), while total enrolments have increased by over one-half. It is claimed that spending per head on health has been reduced by 50%, and on education by 25%, in the 37 poorest nations over the last few years (UNICEF 1989).

However, these figures cover only central government expenditure while some countries have been decentralising both operations and financing to local authorities. In both Tanzania and Zambia, for example, the share of central government expenditure going to education and health has fallen almost by half, from 25/26% in 1972 to 13/14% in 1987, but a large part of this drop can be accounted for by the transfer of responsibility to district level.

There is more direct evidence available of cut-backs and their effects on input indicators. A major UNICEF study showed that expenditure per capita on health and education fell sharply in a large number of countries in Africa and Latin America in the early 1980s and there was a general decrease in government expenditure on food subsidies in real terms (Pinstrup-Andersen et al 1987). The falls in expenditure per capita were more widespread in Latin America than Africa; Latin American countries also cut education more, while African countries cut health more.

Health

The evidence of resulting deterioration was clearest in relation to health and nutrition. For example, in Sri Lanka, per capita daily calorie consumption of the bottom 20 per cent of the population

54

fell by around 10% (Sahn 1987) in the late 1970s/early 1980s and there was a large increase (from 6.1% to 9.4%) in nutritional wasting among children in rural areas (Cornia 1987). In Zambia, increasing child malnutrition was reflected in almost a doubling of hospital admissions and an increasing mortality rate (from 15% to 19%) in the early to mid 1980s, as the degree of malnutrition became more severe (Clark 1988). In Brazil, infant mortality worsened after a long decline, especially in the North-East where the effects of the recession were compounded by a major drought (Pfefferman 1987).

However, despite budget cuts, continuing advances have been made in primary health care throughout the 1980s. For example, the proportion of children in the developing world protected by immunisation has been increased from under 15% to over 80% in this decade, thus saving the lives of over 12 million children (UNICEF 1991). Similarly, the proportion of children with diarrhoea being treated with oral rehydration therapy has gone up from less than 1% in 1980 to almost one-quarter, thus preventing up to one million deaths per year. There has also been a build-up and maintenance of centres of health knowledge and social organisation and practice, e.g. levels of mothers' education, hygiene customs and traditional health practices (Cornia 1984). However, some 14 million children are still dying each year from common illnesses and undernutrition, most of which could be prevented by relatively simple, low-cost methods (UNICEF 1989).

Education

In the education sector, there is evidence of declining primary school enrolment rates, increasing drop-out rates and losses of qualified teachers (Cornia 1987). For example, in Tanzania, gross enrolment in primary education fell from 104 in 1979 to 66 in 1987 (*World Development Reports*) – ratios can exceed 100% because many students are older than the country's standard primary school age. In 21 out of 33 countries for which figures were available, expenditure per primary school pupil fell, often steeply, in the early 1980s (UNICEF 1989).

Overall

Although there is some evidence of deterioration in basic needs availability, the argument that "the march of human progress has now become a retreat" (UNICEF 1989) applies only to a limited number of countries, or particular sub-groups of the population. The overall picture is still one of broad social advance, which seems difficult to reconcile with the deterioration in economic circumstances in the 1980s. A number of arguments can be put forward to explain these divergent trends in the economic and social indicators.

Firstly, as argued earlier, the rapid economic growth in many countries in the 1960s and 1970s did not always bring concomitant improvement in social indicators, thus it is not surprising that there is no direct correlation on the downswing either. Secondly, there was no correlation in the past between levels of social expenditure and improvement in basic needs, because of inequities in distribution. Thirdly, the level of aggregation of many of the indicators (i.e. national averages) may conceal serious deterioration among particular%% vulnerable groups. Fourthly, there may be significant time-lags, partly because of delays in collecting and analysing statistics, and partly because cuts are often translated first into a decline in the quality of services rather than in their absolute contraction so that the impact is not apparent in the short-term (Cornia 1984).

Chapter 4

Factors Affecting Performance on Basic Needs

There is great diversity in achievements on basic needs; life expectancy in the low-income countries, for example, ranges from 42 years in Sierra Leone to over 70 in Sri Lanka, and under-five mortality from almost 30% of live births in Afghanistan to under 5% in China. There has been a noticeable trend for the better-off developing countries to advance faster, with the poorest countries being left behind on welfare as well as monetary indicators (Nissan and Caveny 1988).

Analysis of performance

A number of studies have examined the differences in performance, in order to identify the type of political and economic strategies that tend to be most successful in meeting basic needs. Life expectancy, infant mortality and literacy have been the most commonly used indicators of achievement. The two principal approaches have been: a) cross section analysis of performance in a wide range of countries; and b) analysis of good and poor performers. The results of these studies are summarised below.

Income levels and growth

As might be expected, the most important variable explaining the average level of basic needs satisfaction is average income (GNP per capita), as material basic needs are ultimately satisfied out of material income (Hopkins and Van Der Hoeven 1983).

Statistical analysis of cross-section data has shown that about 70 per cent of variation in life expectancy can be explained by differences in average per capita incomes (Stewart 1985), but the connection is not invariable. Thus, countries like China and Sri Lanka have achieved high average levels of life expectancy (around 70 years) and low under-5 mortality rates (43) at per capita income levels of around $300-400, while countries such as

Brazil and Mexico, with average per capita incomes over $2,000, are still short of such levels.

There are divergent findings for different groups of countries, with significant correlations between social indicators and per capita incomes in low income countries but none for middle income countries; correlations with income distribution are found only for middle income countries (Leipziger and Lewis 1980). Thus, at lower levels of per capita income, growth appears to be necessary for progress on basic needs. However, at higher levels of income, once a critical level of development has been achieved, it is distributional factors which play the major role. Although income distribution did not appear to be an important determinant of average levels of basic needs performance, it is clearly important for the satisfaction of the basic needs of the poorest groups.

The statistical correlations between income levels and basic needs achievement are consistent both with the "trickle down" argument, whereby economic growth leads to basic needs achievement (Stewart 1985), and the "trickle up" argument, whereby social development is a cause of subsequent economic growth (Newman and Thompson 1989). Other studies suggest that economic expansion requires, among other things, a minimal degree of basic needs satisfaction to start with and that economic development lags some 10-20 years behind social development (Weidemann and Muller 1984). However, no significant correlations were found between social and economic indicators in Africa, even when time lags were taken into consideration (Sangmeister 1987).

There is no evidence of any conflict between economic growth and basic needs achievement – in fact, there is some evidence that a basic needs emphasis in development can be instrumental in increasing the rate of growth (Hicks 1979). It is often hypothesised that a high growth strategy requires high investment and a certain degree of inequality, while basic needs achievement is normally assumed to require high social expenditure and a high degree of equality. In practice, basic needs achievers did not have lower investment ratios, nor higher ratios of public consumption, nor markedly more equality, nor is the converse true of those countries performing badly in relation to basic needs (Stewart 1985).

Similarly, there is no evidence of any conflict between industrialisation and basic needs achievement. Thus it is possible to meet the more pressing basic needs, even at fairly low levels of per capita income, without sacrificing growth (Burki and Ul Haq 1981).

58   *Bread and Freedom*

Development strategies

Countries showing especially good progress on basic needs fall into three broad categories (Stewart 1985):

1) Socialist countries, including Albania, China, Cuba and Mongolia;
2) Market-oriented countries, with rapid and labour-absorbing economic growth, including Hong Kong, Korea and Taiwan; and
3) Mixed economies, with welfare state-type interventions, including Costa Rica and Sri Lanka.

In the socialist countries, the planning of production was the leading aspect while a more egalitarian distribution of income (plus rationing) ensured a satisfactory allocation of basic needs goods and services. In the successful capitalist economies, public sector provision of education and health services played an essential role, alongside the growth of private incomes. In the case of the welfare state successes, government interventions operated both with respect to production (especially the provision of public services) and incomes (through subsidies). What is common to a number of these widely divergent countries is a fairly equitable distribution of physical assets, particularly land, and a decentralisation of administration and decision-making to the local level, with adequate central support (Burki and Ul Haq 1981).

A large number of the countries with the poorest performance in relation to basic needs are to be found in Sub-Saharan Africa. They include mixed (primarily capitalist) economies, such as Nigeria and South Africa, and semi-socialist countries such as Angola and Ethiopia. They include countries that have experienced fairly rapid economic growth (e.g. Ivory Coast) and those whose per capita income has declined (e.g. Zambia).

In addition to the inadequacy of material resources, a general feature of many of the poor performers is organisational deficiencies (Stewart 1985). Thus the household sector is weak, mainly because of lack of education; the organisation of the public sector is inadequate to meet basic needs, especially in the rural areas; and a weak private sector means heavy dependence on imported managers and technology, with little spread of employment and other income-earning opportunities. In some countries, special factors have influenced their performance on basic needs, e.g. apartheid policies in South Africa, war in Ethiopia and Angola.

Another group of poor performers are the oil-rich and other mineral dependent countries (e.g. Bolivia, Iran and Libya), where incomes are concentrated and development is not widely diffused.

Public expenditure

Raising the incomes of the poor requires broadly based economic growth, but making the poor better off in other respects, e.g. by reducing child mortality, can be brought about through specific public actions (World Bank 1990). For example, it has been estimated that it would have taken Sri Lanka somewhere between 58 and 152 years, depending on assumptions, to achieve its current high level of life expectancy primarily through growth, rather than through direct public action (Sen 1981).

However, emphasis on social expenditure has not always meant emphasis on basic needs. Thus, figures for total central government expenditure on health and education show no association with basic needs performance for either low or middle-income countries (Stewart 1985). Similarly, the proportion of public expenditure going to defence was not correlated (positively or negatively) with the basic needs performance. In many countries, the biggest obstacle was not the absence of resources but political restraints on their use by entrenched interests (Burki and Ul Haq 1981).

In many cases basic needs have remained unmet, not because public expenditure on them has been insufficient, but because it has been misdirected and has not benefitted all population groups. In Brazil, for instance, the proportion of public health expenditure devoted to preventive medicine declined from 87 per cent in 1949 to under 30 per cent in 1975 (Burki 1980). Similar distortions are found in the education sector; in Pakistan, for example, 40 per cent of the education budget went to the universities which accounted for only 3 per cent of the student body.

Although there are many examples of inappropriate allocations of public expenditures, the evidence shows that the countries which have succeeded in providing primary education and health care to the poor are those that have made adequate provision for the purpose in their budgets (World Bank 1990). Thus, it is clear that even low-income countries can dramatically improve social services through well-directed public expenditures.

Sectoral priorities

Despite differences in methodology, coverage and timing, there is considerable agreement between the different studies as to the most important instruments/inputs for raising life expectancy. Basic education, as measured either by literacy rates or enrolment

60

ratios, emerged as the top priority in all cross-country and cross-sectoral analyses, with female education being especially significant (Stewart 1985). Both a priori reasoning and some statistical tests suggest that the main direction of causality is likely to be from education to health and life expectancy (Burki and Ul Haq 1981). For example, differences in literacy were found to account (statistically) for a significant part of observed differences in child mortality in Mexico (Wood 1988).

There is also agreement in the literature that neither the average availability of calories per capita nor the percentage access to clean water is significantly associated with life expectancy (Stewart 1985). As regards calorie availability, it obviously depends upon the distribution of the available food between and within households. There are similar distribution questions in relation to expenditure on water and sanitation, e.g. only 14% of the benefits of World Bank water and sanitation projects are believed to go to those in absolute poverty (Burki and Ul Haq 1981). Education can substitute for improvements in the quality of water, as it appears to have done in Sri Lanka, if people are taught to boil water to eliminate contamination. Nutrition education and instruction in hygiene and sanitation can also substitute for some basic health services.

An important lesson to emerge from the range of sector studies on basic needs is that cross-sectoral linkages and appropriate substitution and phasing are crucial, both to improve results and reduce costs. For example, parental schooling is positively associated with child health and nutrition (Wolfe and Behrman 1982), while education and better nutrition of adults helps to raise farm productivity (Strauss 1986).

The second lesson is that human attitudes and motivation, and social institutions, administration and organisation are as important as adequate physical, financial and fiscal resources and appropriate technology (Streeten et al 1981). The third lesson is that a successful approach depends heavily on the contribution of women (Burki and Ul Haq 1981). For example, childhood survival in all major regions of the developing world is highly sensitive to the length of formal schooling of the mother. Even after adjustment for economic factors, 1-3 years of schooling is associated with a fall of 20% in childhood risk of death and further large decreases are recorded with successive increments in educational attainment (Cleland and Van Ginneken 1989).

Apart from these broad conclusions, the studies show that countries can meet basic needs in a variety of ways and that there are no iron laws which must be followed (Hicks 1982).

Liberties and rights

There is evidence that those developing countries whose citizens enjoyed greater political and civil liberties also performed better in terms of improvements in life expectancy, infant survival rates and per capita incomes (Dasgupta 1989). Other analysts have found significant relationships between per capita incomes and civil and political rights (Pritchard 1989). In general, countries ranking high on the UNDP's Human Development Index have more democratic political and social frameworks than the poor performers, with some notable exceptions (UNDP 1990).

Thus, the argument that poor nations cannot afford the luxury of civil and political rights is belied by their own experience. Similarly, there is some evidence for a positive relationship between basic needs performance and indices of participation: "increased participation does not necessarily hamper the satisfaction of other basic needs and, conversely, the pursuit of material progress is no argument at all for denying democratic rights" (Hopkins and Van Der Hoeven 1983).

For the UNDP, "Freedom ...is the most vital component of human development strategies" (UNDP 1990). People must be free to participate actively in economic and political life, thus, ensuring that social goals do not become mechanical devices in the hands of paternalistic governments. Only economic and social rights put people in a position to implement freedom for themselves (Moltmann 1990).

The variety of ways in which basic needs can be promoted is both a strength and a problem in relation to making their achievement a human right (Stewart 1988). It is a strength because it means that different types of society can succeed without having to change fundamental features of their political economy, such as the ownership of assets and the organisation of production. It is a problem because it means that there are no simple ways of identifying whether a society is going about it in the "right" way. For example, it is not possible to say a priori that food subsidies are or are not essential – it depends on the whole structure of the economic and political systems, as well as cultural and sociological factors in particular countries.

Basic needs and growth

There have been contrasting approaches to the improvement of welfare and the amelioration of poverty at different times and in different places. They can be divided into a **direct** or basic needs approach and an **indirect** or economic growth approach. The primary distinction is between creating income, and hence consumption, and providing consumption, in kind or through income transfers (Bhagwati 1988). The optimal policy for any country would generally involve a mix of the two approaches.

In the 1950s and 1960s, the growth-based indirect route to attacking poverty was the most fashionable. In the 1970s, it was increasingly argued that the indirect route was ineffective and the basic needs strategy was put forward as the appropriate direct route. By the 1980s, the growth-based route came to be seen in a more favourable light, but the emphasis shifted to adjustment, ostensibly to create the conditions for future sustained growth.

Emerging consensus

The battle between the direct and indirect approaches is gradually giving way to an emerging consensus that both are important and even complementary in many ways (Isenman 1987). Thus, there is now little support for the simplistic version of the basic needs strategy that relegated growth to a minor role. On the other hand, the basic needs approach has contributed to an increased recognition that growth alone is not a sufficient objective or measure of development strategies, and that steps to meet basic health and educational needs can contribute to increasing incomes and reducing the rate of population growth.

For example, there is now firm evidence that better nutrition raises farm productivity and rural wages, both in Africa (Strauss 1986) and Asia (Behrman et al 1988). World Bank studies, amongst others, have produced strong evidence that education also improves a farmer's efficiency – when the increase resulting from education was compared with the costs, rates of return compared very favourably with other sectors (World Bank 1980). The fact that labour markets respond to human capital accumulation emphasises the importance of investments in education and nutrition in reducing poverty (Sahn and Alderman 1988).

Thus, a recent *World Development Report* (World Bank 1990) argues for a two-part strategy to achieve rapid and politically sustainable progress on poverty. The first is to encourage a pattern of growth that makes efficient use of labour and the second is to provide basic social services to the poor. The two elements are seen as mutually reinforcing; promoting the productive use of labour furnishes opportunities for the poor, while investment in health and education improves their immediate well-being and enables them to take advantage of the opportunities.

Even if this basic strategy were adopted, many of the world's poor would continue to experience severe deprivation, so well-targeted transfers and safety nets would also be required. As argued by UNDP, "the chronically deprived and dispossessed must be brought up to a threshold of human development to enter the mainstream of economic growth" (UNDP 1990).

Potential conflicts

It is increasingly recognised that a significant part of spending, operating as well as capital, on human development is investment (World Bank 1980). However, a harmony of interests between human resource developers and humanitarians cannot be taken for granted. Choices have to be made, and the decision may depend on whether humanitarianism or productivity is the overriding concern (Streeten 1984). For example, conflicts may arise with respect to the beneficiaries (e.g. members of the labour force or the old and/or sick), the content of programmes (e.g. general education or technical training) or the constituencies (e.g. official agencies or NGOs). Thus, a pure basic needs approach may conflict at times with a productivity and growth approach, although the two overlap to a substantial extent.

The recent African blueprint for sustainable development emphasises that "..development has to be engineered and sustained by the people themselves through their full and active participation ...To achieve and sustain development, it is necessary to ensure the education and training, health, well-being and vitality of the people so that they can participate fully and effectively in the development process" (ECA 1989).

Chapter 5

Basic Needs and Human Rights

Introduction

Human rights can be divided into into three categories, or generations. The first generation are the civil and political rights, often described as "negative" rights as they are concerned with non-interference with individual liberties. A second generation of "positive" rights, includes economic, social and cultural rights, which involve claims to something, e.g. food, health care and work. The third generation are collective rights, or "rights of solidarity", such as rights to development, a healthy environment, and peace.

Positive rights are inevitably asserted to scarce goods and so there is a limit on their claim, while it is argued that negative rights do not have such natural limitations (Dasgupta 1989).

Universal Declarations and Legal Covenants

The Universal Declaration of Human Rights, adopted by the United Nations in 1948, incorporated economic, social, cultural, civil and political rights. For example, Article 25 states that "Everyone has a right to a standard of living adequate for the health and well-being of himself and of his family, including food, clothing, housing and medical care and necessary social services", while the following article (26) declares that "Everyone has the right to education".

It was only in 1966 that the legally non-binding resolution was followed up by two International Covenants on Civil and Political Rights and on Economic, Social and Cultural Rights, which translate the ideals or moral norms of the Universal Declaration into enforceable legal norms. It was a further 10 years before they were ratified by a sufficient number of countries to come into force. The Covenants have now been accepted by the majority of UN members (92 and 87 respectively as of 1989); Ireland only ratified them towards the end of 1989.

Each of the Covenants imposes different legal obligations on ratifying states. In relation to civil and political rights, there is an immediate obligation to comply with the provisions of the covenant. By comparison, a state party to the Economic, Social and Cultural Rights Covenant only "undertakes to take steps... to the maximum of its available resources, with a view to achieving progressively the full realization of the rights recognised." It is argued by some that the civil and political rights are mainly safeguards while the economic, social and cultural rights are mainly aspirations, though widely accepted (De Kadt 1980).

Two key assumptions underlay the arguments originally advanced in favour of separating the two categories of rights into two distinct treaties with different obligations for implementation (Jhabvala 1984). The first was that national governments were the major violators of human rights. The second was that all civil and political rights were easily implemented through relatively simple legislative and administrative measures without the expenditure of resources and that they all required state abstention rather than activism.

However, the implementation of civil and political rights requires "affirmative action" and this involves the use of scarce resources. At the same time, powerful economic, ethnic, religious or other groups within societies may be major violators of human rights, despite the best efforts of relatively weak governments. Thus, the implementation of civil and political rights also depends very much upon the socio-economic context.

Right to development

In 1986, a non-binding "Declaration on the Right to Development" was adopted by the UN General Assembly. The United States was the only country to vote against it, although other industrialised countries had misgivings; the idea that states, as well as individuals, should have a right to development gave rise to some controversy.

In the Declaration, development was described as "a comprehensive economic, social, cultural and political process, which aimed at the constant improvement of the well-being of the entire population and of all individuals on the basis of their active, free and meaningful participation in development and in the fair distribution of benefits resulting therefrom".

In order to promote the realisation of the right to development, states have, inter alia, the following duties:

- to pay equal attention to both categories of human rights (civil/political and economic/social/cultural); and

- to ensure that every human being has an equal opportunity in access to basic needs.

Complementarity

In the same way that growth came to dominate development thinking, concern with civil and political rights issues came to dominate human rights endeavours (Alston 1981). However, the UN doctrine is that "equal attention and urgent consideration should be given to the implementation, promotion and protection of both civil and political, and economic, social and cultural rights" (Resolution 32/130, 1977).

The second basic concept put forward in this resolution is that "The full realization of civil and political rights without the enjoyment of economic, social and cultural rights is impossible; the achievement of lasting progress in the implementation of human rights is dependent upon sound and effective national and international policies of economic and social development".

The objectives of the basic needs strategy have much in common with human rights objectives, at least in terms of certain economic and social rights, such as those relating to education, food, health care and housing. On the other hand, civil and political rights are only dealt with by the basic needs approach in so far as they are included in the strategy's concern for participation in decision-making (Alston 1979).

The major advantage of making human rights objectives an integral part of the basic needs strategy would be to provide the latter with a comprehensive and acceptable ethical base. At the same time, basic needs could be a mechanism for promoting the broader concept of economic, social and cultural rights. On the other hand, the objective of meeting basic needs might attract more support on its own than in association with traditional human rights objectives (Alston 1979).

The liberal view that human rights and basic needs complement each other is considered by some to be more an article of faith than a statement of a necessary connection (Vincent 1986). In some countries, the record on meeting basic needs is relatively good but that on civil and political rights relatively bad (e.g. China); in other countries (e.g. India) these records are reversed.

Material needs can be met in ways which conflict with rights, e.g. "If society were organised benevolently, like a zoo, or less benevolently, like a well-run prison, physical needs would be met at a high level, but human rights would be denied" (Streeten et al 1981). On the other hand, the principle of one person – one vote might conflict with the satisfaction of basic needs; for example, if entrenched interests were in a position to frustrate the rights of minorities. Thus, basic needs can be met in ways which deny human rights and human rights can be practiced in ways which reject basic needs.

The vagueness of the economic and social rights (e.g. "adequate food"), especially when contrasted with the elaborate precision of most civil and political rights, has tended to encourage their relative neglect (Eide 1989). The more recent stress on economic and social rights has promoted the view that the right to life is as much about providing the wherewithal to sustain life as protecting it against violence – a positive right requiring action by others as well as a negative right requiring merely non-interference.

The emergence of the doctrine of basic needs may be interpreted as marking the reception of the force of this idea by the international community (Alston 1981). If there is a right to life, which is a right to subsistence as well as security, then such a right also implies correlative obligations, on national states and on the international community.

Cultural relativism

Human rights embody many tenets found in all the world's cultures, but the theoretical origins of the human rights movement are considered to be distinctively Western. Though historically they may have been better articulated in certain societies than in others, human rights are not peculiar to or valid only in those societies, any more than mathematical, logical or scientific principles have their validity only in those societies where they were originally articulated (Maduagwu 1987).

In many cultures, rights are closely linked to duties and may only attach to certain groups, e.g. "true believers", members of the caste or tribe. For example, in the 1977 USSR Constitution, the exercise of rights and liberties was stated to be "inseparable from the performance by citizens of their duties" (Article 59). The social and political doctrines of Islam reflect a strong concern for human good and human dignity, but the emphasis is on duties rather than rights. Similarly, in Confucian China, traditional doctrine was expressed almost entirely in terms of the duties of the ruler. Until the middle of the twentieth century, the Christian churches as a whole also experienced great difficulties in coming to acknowledge human rights (Walf 1990).

The socio-economic and cultural context may affect the particular formulation and emphasis of rights concepts in different cultures. Thus, basic needs, like basic rights, attach to **individuals** in Western thinking; the Third World, on the other hand, often argues for the primacy of **national** needs and national rights. For example, the Organisation of African Unity adopted a "Charter on Human and People's Rights" in 1981, while the recently signed Convention between the European Community and its ACP (African, Caribbean and Pacific) partners also includes an article on "Human and People's Rights". South Asian societies such as India tend to recognise the individual only as part of a community ordering (Kothari 1989); Hindus also criticise Western conceptions of rights as too human-centred and neglecting the totality of living creatures (Rubin 1989). There is a continuing need for such Third World insights into human rights issues, but as a process of supplementation and not derogation (Coomaraswamy 1982).

Human rights, as they are understood today, were first crystalised in the Western world because of historical factors, but parallel approaches were adopted in various parts of the world (Saksena 1989). The much greater individualism of the Western human rights approach results in part from particular social and political conditions. As modernisation and development increasingly sever individuals in other societies from their traditional small, supportive communities, then, regardless of how one views this process, the human rights approach may be seen as a logical and necessary evolution of the means for realising human dignity (Donnelly 1982).

Needs and rights

The language of wants, needs and rights tends to be emotional and somewhat subjective. Thus, **wants** are morally neutral, though sometimes regarded as greedy; there is a strong implication that **needs** ought to be fulfilled, while **rights** connote a stronger moral, and also legal, imperative (Stewart 1988).

The market system is premised on "consumers' sovereignty" which means giving priority to meeting the desires/wants of those with purchasing power; obviously, this need not lead to the fulfilment of basic needs for all. Total reliance on the market would imply a value-judgement that the satisfaction of anyone's preferences takes priority over the satisfaction of everyone's basic needs (Weigel 1986). Few would argue for the total replacement of the market mechanism, but rather for its supplementation in relation to certain basic goods and services.

The emphasis must be on "basic human needs", whereby people participate both in defining their own needs and in meeting them. It is necessary to go further and to ensure the acceptance of basic needs as a doctrine of human rights imposing correlative obligations, and not merely as one option in the strategy of development. This would increase the moral imperative and political commitment to the fulfilment of basic needs and would give them some international legal status, the extent of which would depend on the supervisory and enforcement mechanisms available (Vincent 1986).

The most far-reaching linkage of development and human rights would be to conceive of development as the progressive satisfaction of all human rights (Zacaquette 1984). "So long as human beings aspire, human rights will be a limitless concept" (Trivedi 1981); thus, they will make progressive and continuous demands on the economic system. However, the establishment of a minimal level of needs satisfaction is an essential prerequisite for the progressive achievement of full human rights standards. At a broader level it is possible to think of an initial "core" of human rights, cutting across the civil rights, the social rights and the recently formulated solidarity rights (De Kadt 1980).

Basic rights

It is possible to identify a set of "basic rights", whose fulfilment seems necessary for the exercise of all rights. In this category would be those civil and political rights which bear directly on physical life, such as security from assault, and on the socio-economic side "the rights to subsistence", such as adequate food, clothing, shelter, health care and safe water. Since the enjoyment of these life-related basic rights is essential to the enjoyment of all other rights, they amount to "everyone's minimal reasonable demands upon the rest of humanity" (Shue 1980). The correlative duties involve not only **respecting** other people's rights, but also **protecting** others from deprivation and **aiding** those incapable of providing for their own needs.

Minimal threshold

The basic needs concept yields a criterion for selecting rights that, if fulfilled, could assure a minimal threshold of well-being (Andreassen et al 1988). The identification of minimalist levels for each right might vary among countries, e.g. nutrition related to body size and climate. A minimum threshold for human rights realisation could be made operational by means of country-specific thresholds, measured by indicators such as nutrition, infant mortality, disease frequency, life expectancy, income, unemployment and underemployment.

70

The scope of violation of socio-economic rights would then refer to the proportion and distribution of the population not assured of this minimal threshold. This approach would call for the identification of the most deprived groups, not only according to the conventional definitions, such as gender, racial and regional, but also distinctions defined by the control over assets, e.g. land-owners on the one hand and labourers or share-croppers on the other (Eide 1989).

Action required

It is clearly on the ground in both developed and developing countries that the principal action is required, i.e. an acceptance of the indivisibility of human rights, a commitment to ensuring equal opportunity in access to basic goods and services and a struggle against vested economic and social interests to achieve these goals. Financial and other support will be needed from a range of outside bodies to assist the poorer countries in particular.

International level

Although human rights is one of the four purposes recognised in the United Nations' Charter, only 0.7% of the organisation's programme budget is allocated to achieve this purpose and the resulting shortage of staff and resources threatens to make a mockery of the implementation machinery under the Covenants (Opsahl 1989). A survey by the UN's Joint Inspection Unit of the achievements and shortcomings of the UN system concluded that the attitude within the organisation on economic, social and cultural rights "remains one of hypocrisy and longwindedness" (Bertrand 1985).

Although human rights is supposed to be an integral part of development policies, the United Nations preaches a theory which it does not practice itself (van Boven 1989). The human rights programme, which is administered by the UN Centre for Human Rights in Geneva, functions separately from the main programmes and agencies. Among the specialised agencies, the ILO (International Labour Organisation) and UNICEF (United Nations Children's Fund) have made a more substantive contribution to the implementation of the Covenant on Economic, Social and Cultural Rights than any of the others. FAO (Food and Agriculture Organisation), WHO (World Health Organisation) and, to a lesser extent, UNESCO (United Nations Education, Scientific and Cultural Organisation) "have demonstrated an almost total lack of interest in contributing to the Covenant's implementation procedures" (Alston 1987).

Within the UN there are different mechanisms for the supervision of the two human rights covenants – on civil and political and economic/social/cultural rights. A special organ, the Human Rights Committee, was created to supervise the implementation of the first covenant but the supervision of the second was delegated to ECOSOC (the Economic and Social Committee). The latter then established a Committee on Economic, Social and Cultural Rights, made up initially of government representatives but, since 1986, consisting of independent experts. Only states have to submit reports about their own policies – the most inadequate aspect of the Covenant's reporting and supervisory procedures is the fact that no provision is made for formal input to be received from NGOs (Alston 1987). However, NGOs could still supply additional information to ensure that the Committee obtained a complete picture of the human rights situation in the reporting country (von Hebel 1989).

At present, enforcement of economic/social/cultural rights depends entirely on publicity associated with the reporting system. This can be an important force, especially when it subsequently influences other countries' policies towards the deviant state. Thus, human rights bodies could help to publicise the work of the Committee, including its shortcomings.

Another enforcement mechanism would be to use the leverage of international financial institutions to ensure compliance; this would be analogous to their present use of leverage to enforce economic reforms. The shift within financial and development institutions from exclusively economic considerations to environmental and ecological concerns might also open the door to human rights concerns (van Boven 1989).

At a minimum, the World Bank (and perhaps the IMF) should assemble statistics on the human condition of the poor for their appraisal of country performance, thus, greatly improving effective monitoring (Stewart 1988). There is a need for evaluative criteria for assessing state activity, e.g. human impact statements analagous to currently used environmental impact statements (Dias 1981). A useful start has been made in this area by the United Nations Development Programme with its new series of annual *Human Development Reports* (UNDP 1990).

The obligations imposed on the international community should also be reviewed and enforced, e.g. as regards resource flows and trading arrangements.

Donors

Western countries should be made more conscious of their duties under the several human rights conventions, especially the duty to cooperate internationally with other countries to promote the realisation of economic, social and cultural rights. They should incorporate human rights considerations in their development' policies and monitor them on a regular basis.

The Parliamentary Assembly of the Council of Europe has argued that "any development cooperation policy must take the human rights situation into consideration" and recommended that member governments should "make it the primary objective of their cooperation and official development aid policies to contribute not only to the satisfaction of basic needs .... but also towards progress in the protection of civil and political rights" (Anon 1982).

A strong poverty focus, combined with clearly defined targets and measurable outputs, would provide a solid base for mobilising public support. As recognised by the Chairman of the OECD's Development Assistance Committee, in his annual report (OECD 1989): "In the eyes of large segments of aid-supporting public opinion in donor countries, helping poor people in poor countries to live more decent lives is the essential rationale for development assistance. While governments have to take a complex range of objectives and foreign policy aims into account in the use of official development assistance, aid effectiveness must in the end be assessed against this standard".

The appropriate technologies now exist for satisfying the basic needs of all the world's population at a reasonable cost – equivalent to around 5% of today's total military spending (UNICEF 1989). This would require an increase of 50% in total aid flows, bringing them to an average of 0.5% of GNP. Of at least equal importance to the increase in total aid would be the specific allocation of a substantial proportion (at least one-third) to poverty-focussed aid. "Real aid" campaigns, already under way in many European countries and in the USA, will be required to ensure that national governments meet these targets, in terms of both volume and quality.

For example, in the USA, the proposed Global Poverty Reduction Act (an initiative of an international NGO lobby) seeks to focus aid on three goals: the reduction of under-five mortality rates to 70 or less, the raising of female literacy rates to 80% or more; and the reduction of the number of people living in absolute poverty to less than 20% in all countries (UNICEF 1989).

Non-governmental organisations (NGOs)

An essential aspect of the evolution of supervision and monitoring in regard to civil and political rights has been the involvement of NGOs, e.g. Amnesty and the International Commission of Jurists, but there are few such international NGOs which address themselves explicitly to economic, social and cultural rights. In relation to the latter, the NGO influence has been mainly at the national or local level.

The voluntary groups and grassroots social movements need an initial measure of freedom to operate and pursue their objectives. Civil and political rights can help protect these movements from repression and are thus, complementary to their struggles to protect economic and social rights through the empowerment of resourceless groups (Rubin 1989).

Third World NGOs

The recent emergence of thousands of voluntary human rights and development groups in Third World countries is perhaps the single most important contemporary force working for increased global respect for international humanitarian principles but these groups remain "unknown, underrated and neglected" (Egeland 1988).

For example, Africa has more than ten thousand formal organisations working for civil and/or socio-economic rights –over a thousand in Kenya alone. There are over 1,000 registered developmental, environmental and civil liberties groups in Brazil and several thousand in each of the South Asian countries. However, there are relatively few civil rights organisations in North Africa or the Middle East as yet.

Local NGOs are an essential part of "the minimum social infrastructure" required for a strong basic needs approach (Wisner 1988). A distinction should be made between macro-policy reform, which can be achieved by pre-emptive central action, and micro-policy reform which depends on complex and difficult institutional changes, e.g. the development of self-reliant local organisations. Micro-level policy reforms are more likely to be achieved through the facilitation of social progress than through legal proclamation (Korten 1987).

The political, social and other constraints on reaching the poor effectively, even where governments genuinely attempt to do so, underlines the importance of the role of voluntary agencies and social action groups (Bhagwati 1988). These groups not only aid the poor directly but also act as watchdogs and assist the poor to secure access to the programmes designed for their benefit. This includes the development of legal resources "to provide access not only to law but also to justice through law by struggling to bring about reform of unjust laws" (Dias 1984).

It is now recognised by the major donors that "If self-reliant, sustained and equitable development is the ultimate goal of development activities, then the role of the aid system is to support and strengthen the institutional capabilities of indigenous NGOs, particularly those which hold special potential for poverty reduction and socio-economic development, such as women's organisations and rural associations" (OECD 1989). A primary goal in supporting indigenous NGOs would be to enable them to define their own objectives, to carry out development activities, to gain access to resources and to make them recognised by their own authorities as partners in development.

Local NGOs would have some comparative advantage in the delivery of basic needs. However, one way to weaken the potential impact of either indigenous or foreign NGOs would be to load them down with mandates to deliver basic needs to the poor while governments and donors proceeded with business as usual (Wisner 1988).

Northern NGOs

Among development NGOs it is possible to identify three generations of strategies and related modes of operation (Korten 1987):

1) Mainly relief and welfare,
2) Small-scale self-reliant local development, and
3) Sustainable systems development at local, national and international levels.

Because of their limited resources, NGOs can only assist a few favoured localities if they are involved in the direct delivery of services. At any rate, the conventional wisdom that NGOs are better than official agencies (whether donors, international financial institutions or public bodies in developing countries) in tackling poverty, stimulating community development and providing disaster and famine relief remains largely untested (ODI 1988a).

At the next level, self-reliant local initiatives require links with supportive national (and international) systems if they are to survive and develop. Thus, northern NGOs are increasingly adopting the third generation strategy, in which they adopt more catalytic and educational roles than operational ones. (All three generations can, and do, co-exist – sometimes even within a single NGO).

On the ground, the main emphasis is likely to be on the building up of the capacity of local NGOs. However, local institution-building has proved difficult for NGOs and many of the difficulties mirror those in the relationship between official donors and governments – "the need to be less dirigiste, to have confidence in local agencies and to move beyond lending for projects to lending in support of broader programmes" (World Bank 1989). Similarly, in relation to official co-financing of NGOs, it is now generally agreed that donors should promote the financing of multi-year programmes which enhance long-term planning and coordination rather than rely on the more traditional fragmented project support (OECD 1989).

A major priority of NGOs must be to campaign for the acceptance at home and abroad of the indivisibility of human rights, whether civil/political or social/economic/cultural, and the putting into practice of this principle. This includes fighting for increased national aid budgets and monitoring the extent to which the programmes constitute "real aid". Another priority is to assist with the collection of micro-level data on a coordinated basis to monitor the impact of economic and social/political developments on vulnerable groups. This data should be published directly and fed to the relevant national and international agencies.

"As in the past, the future effectiveness of the NGO community lies not in changing fashion but in fashioning change" (Brodhead 1987).

Chapter 6

Basic Needs Prospects and Policy Challenges

Economic outlook

The World Bank has prepared forecasts for growth prospects in the 1990s. Its projected growth rates for real GDP per capita in different regions are summarised below and compared with past trends.

Table 6.1 Real GDP per capita growth rates % p.a.

Country Group	Past Trends 1965-80	Past Trends 1980-89	Projected 1989-2000
All developing	3.4	2.3	3.2
Sub-Saharan Africa	2.0	-2.2	0.5
East Asia (incl China)	4.8	6.7	5.1
South Asia (incl India)	1.2	3.2	3.2
L. America/Caribbean	3.4	-0.6	2.3
Mid. East/N. Africa	3.9	0.8	2.1
Industrial Countries	2.8	2.5	2.6

Source: *World Development Report 1990* (World Bank)

Thus, the Asian development record is expected to continue and some growth in incomes is projected for Latin America and the Caribbean. Debt relief would further boost the growth prospects of highly indebted countries (e.g. Argentina, Brazil, Mexico and Nigeria) in particular. However, with rapid population growth in Sub-Saharan Africa, per capita real incomes are expected to increase only marginally. Even with an optimistic view of adjustment, average incomes in Africa will be no higher by the year 2000 than they were in the late 1960s.

Poverty

There are varying definitions, measurements and projections of poverty in both high and low-income countries. Of particular interest in this context is the basic needs poverty line calculated by ILO staff (Hopkins and Van Der Hoeven 1983). This was derived by choosing targets for food, education, health and housing and calculating per capita income levels required to satisfy these needs. [Housing was always the last need to be satisfied, as with the current higher income countries (Cohen 1986)]. The numbers falling below this poverty line were calculated, inter alia, for the early 1980s and projected to the year 2000. Since the projections were based on the assumption that earlier growth rates would continue, they must now be considered as an underestimate of future poverty levels.

The following table summarises the estimates for 1982 and the projections for the year 2000.

Table 6.2 Extent of basic needs poverty, 1982 and 2000

	Number (mn)		Proportion %	
	1982	2000	1982	2000
Sub-Saharan Africa	200	215	54	37
Asia (excl. China)	788	766	60	39
Near East/N. Africa	36	26	18	8
L. America/Caribbean	86	74	23	13
Total (incl S Europe)	1,114	1,083	47	30

Source: Hopkins and Van Der Hoeven (1983)

The above figures exclude China, where it is estimated that 10% of the rural population are below the absolute poverty level (UNICEF 1989), implying that perhaps 20% (200 million people) would be below the basic needs poverty line. Thus, some 1,300 million people, or one-third of the developing world's population, do not have sufficient incomes to meet their basic needs. The absolute number is expected to decline somewhat by the year 2000, but they would still constitute up to one-quarter of the population of the developing world (including China). Asia would continue to account for three-quarters of the world's poorest people.

Alternative projections

Recent World Bank estimates of the incidence of poverty in 1985 and projections for the year 2000 are summarised below.

Apart from the different base year, these World Bank estimates differ from the basic needs poverty estimates in two important respects:

a)   a more restrictive definition of the poverty line, and

b) relatively optimistic assumptions (except in the case of Africa) about the prospects for labour-intensive growth and provision of social services and "what the two together might achieve" (World Bank 1990).

Table 6.3 Numbers and proportions in poverty, 1985 and 2000

	Number (mn)		Proportion %	
	1985	2000	1985	2000
Sub-Saharan Africa	180	265	47	43
Asia (excl China)	595	400	44	21
China	210	35	20	3
Mid East/N. Africa	60	60	31	23
L. America/Caribbean	75	60	19	11
Total*	1,120	820	33	18

Source: Adapted from World Bank 1990
* Including S Europe, but excluding E Europe

However, the *World Development Report* goes on to recognise that, on less optimistic assumptions about the international environment and domestic policies, the projected figures for the year 2000 could be more than 200 million higher (i.e. India +115 mln, China +70 mln and Latin America +25 mln). This would bring the total back to over one billion, or at least one in five of the population in the Third World.

Nutrition

Projections of undernutrition suggest a sharp drop in the proportion of those undernourished, but a slight increase in the absolute numbers. FAO estimates of undernutrition (below 1.4 times the basal metabolic rate or roughly 1660 calories on average) for the early 1980s and projections to the year 2000 are shown below – China is not included because of the unavailability of data.

Table 6.4 Estimates of undernutrition, 1980 and 2000

	Numbers (mn)		% of population	
	1979/81	2000	1979/81	2000
Sub-Saharan Africa	110	194	31	29
Near East/N. Africa	25	29	11	8
Asia (excl. China)	288	246	24	14
Latin America	52	62	15	12
Total (excl. China)	475	532	22	16

Source: FAO (1987)

Thus, allowing for some continuing problems in China, the number of undernourished people could remain around 600 million, or 12% of the Third World population by the year 2000. The problem of undernutrition is expected to continue to shift from Asia to Africa, where the share of the population undernourished in 2000 will be little below that of the pre-drought 1979/81 period while the absolute numbers could increase by three-quarters. Improved distribution of income and of access to available food supplies would help improve the situation, though not by much in the countries with very low average food availability (FAO 1987).

Infant mortality

The United Nations has adopted as a target for the year 2000 to bring down the Under-5 Mortality Rate to 70 or less in each country, or to half the 1980 level, whichever is the lower. If achieved this would have the effect of reducing the number of child deaths from 14 million per year to 7 million (UNICEF 1991).

Seventeen developing countries (including China) had already brought their rates down to this level by 1980 and a further 24 are on course to reach the target by the year 2000. This implies that under half of the more populous developing countries will meet the target on schedule. Future declines in mortality are projected to be similar to the past (United Nations 1988), in which case the developing countries as a group will not reach the UN target until the year 2015 or thereabouts. On current trends, Africa would not reach this level until about 2050.

The human implication of these projections is that 4 million more children will be dying in the year 2000 than if the UN target were reached. It must also be remembered that the target is not particularly ambitious – an under-five mortality rate of 70, over six times that currently experienced in Ireland.

Implications and options

Despite substantial past and continuing progress on many economic and social indicators, the projections suggest that up to one-quarter of the developing world's population will have inadequate incomes to meet their basic needs in the year 2000 and around half of this number (600 million people) will lack the most basic need, adequate food. The process of differentiation must be expected to continue, with Africa and, to a lesser extent, South Asia (especially India) accounting for the largest concentrations of the poor and undernourished.

If "only" 10-20% are "ultra-poor", it would be feasible even in a low-income country to benefit them with affordable, targetted programmes of growth and/or redistribution (Lipton 1988). For example, as regards food availability, the aggregate energy deficit in most countries is far less than 10 per cent of the food supply (World Bank 1986). However, studies show that the normal course of development, even with a vigorous expansion of food production, is not likely to solve the nutrition problem (e.g. Reutlinger and Alderman 1980).

Thus, there is a need for special measures which improve the income distribution and for interventions in food markets designed to provide for the nutritional needs of the target population. Even an international organisation like FAO has recognised that "There is now a large measure of agreement that there is no real substitute for a change in the ownership of production assets, particularly land, in order to reduce rural poverty" (FAO 1987).

Finance required

Many of the problems of health and nutrition, food and water, housing and education are susceptible to low-cost solutions which have already been tried and tested. Recent development experience suggests that national level action in all the main areas of basic needs is now possible at reasonable cost (UNICEF 1989). Thus, UNICEF argues for making the 1990s into a "Decade for Doing the Obvious".

UNICEF has calculated that the additional financial resources required to meet the most essential of human needs by the year 2000 would be $30-$50 billion per year, i.e. around 5% of today's total military spending (UNICEF 1989). Primary health care could be made available at a cost of around $5 per person per year and primary education or adult literacy programmes for $25 per participant. Similarly, piped water supply and basic sanitation could be made available for an annualised cost of approximately $6 per person.

As much as 25% of total costs could be borne by the communities themselves, with another 25% coming from the reallocation of existing government resources, but external aid would be required to meet the remaining 50%. This could be met by increasing total aid from the current level of around $50 billion to $75 billion, while ensuring that at least one-third of that was allocated to meeting the most essential needs of the poorest groups (UNICEF 1989). The other two-thirds could be used to finance investment (and, in some cases, current consumption) benefitting the population as a whole. Total aid would then be equivalent to around 0.5% of donor nations' GNP, as opposed to the UN target of 0.7%, but the lower target is related to an identified set of outputs, while the UN figure is not.

[For Ireland this would mean almost a tripling of the current aid level in relation to GNP, to a total of around £120 million at current GNP and price levels, i.e. substantially less than annual expenditure on the National Lottery.]

Sustainability

Although external aid could play a key role in providing the initial basic needs facilities and services, the question of their sustainability remains problematic, as up to two-thirds of the total costs are recurrent (Streeten and Burki 1978). The funds required must, in the longer term, be generated from increased economic activity and/or from redistribution in the developing countries themselves, but their opportunities are constrained by external factors.

A substantial part of expenditure on basic needs can be seen as investment in human capital, rather than consumption, so it must be expected to give rise to subsequent increases in productivity and output. However, there may be substantial time lags (generations rather than years in some cases), so that external funding may be required for a long period.

The objectives of the basic needs strategy must be seen, not merely in terms of feeding, clothing and sheltering individuals today and tomorrow, but in terms of enabling all people to ensure their own well-being in the years to come and to realise their full potential. If it is to be more than a large-scale welfare exercise, it must also involve the creation of conditions conducive to long-term development including respect for human rights (Alston 1979).

The development debate

After a decade of "adjustment", there are signs that basic needs is reemerging as a major issue in the development debate, at least as regards the poorest countries. UNICEF first called for "adjustment with a human face" in the early 1980s but now argues that the focus must gradually give way to "development with a human face" (UNICEF 1990). Similarly, a recent World Bank report on Sub-Saharan Africa "strongly supports the call for a human-centred development strategy made by the ECA and UNICEF" (World Bank 1989).

The African "Blueprint for Sustainable Development" (ECA 1989) emphasises "human-centred development", a concept which is said to encompass "essential needs and aspects such as individual freedom and political liberty". It argues that action must be started now on at least a minimally defined set of needs that have to be satisfied in the shortest possible time – "certain basic goods and services such as food, potable water, shelter, primary health care and sanitation, education and cheap transport". In the foreword, it is recognised that "it is only through the motivation and the empowerment of people as well as the ensuring of the equitable distribution of income that development can take place on a sustainable basis" (Adedeji 1989).

Similarly, one leading Arab economist (and Chairman of the Third World Forum) has argued that "there is no shame for us, Third World citizens, in proclaiming the top priority in our development strategy is that the destitute or deprived that often constitute the majority of the population should be secured the minimal satisfaction of their needs" (Abdalla 1986).

The new emphasis results in part from a relearning of the basic lesson that a minimum level of social development must precede economic development, rather than emerging as a subsequent by-product. A study by the United Nations Industrial Development Organisation (UNIDO 1984) concluded that: "Strategies for long-term industrialization in the developing countries should be conceived from a broader perspective in which considerably more attention must be given to the effects which improvements in nutrition, health, education, communication and housing in the present might have on economic growth in the future".

Similarly, the battle between the direct and indirect (via incomes) approaches to basic needs fulfilment is giving way to an emerging consensus that both approaches are important and in many ways complementary. The presumption of market failure and of public sector success was the dominant fashion in development economics for an extended period, but there is now a better appreciation of the relative strengths and weaknesses of both. Experience has shown that public sector goods (e.g. education and health) can be appropriated for the benefit of privileged minorities just as easily as privately produced goods and services.

At the same time, it is recognised that the success of policies aimed at improving the "pull-up" effects of the growth process is critically dependent upon the extent to which "countervailing power" is available to the poor, e.g. through social action groups and political parties (Bhagwati 1988). For those at the bottom of the social structure, growth will rarely facilitate entitlement to basic economic rights without political empowerment (Howard 1989). There may also be conflicts over priorities between the human resource developers (focussing on productivity and growth) and the humanitarians (emphasising basic needs for all).

Lessons of experience

Substantial progress on basic needs has been achieved in a wide range of countries and the better performers have exhibited a variety of political systems and development strategies (see Chapter 4). A good basic needs performance does not require extreme achievements with respect to either income distribution or economic growth, although these may be desired for other reasons. Thus, they are potentially within the reach of most types of economy (Stewart 1985). However, the most successful countries have had a fairly equitable distribution of physical assets, particularly land. They have also displayed a strong and sustained commitment to public programmes in health, education and nutrition (Caldwell 1986).

There is no evidence of conflict between basic needs and economic growth – in fact, investment in the human resource is a necessary precondition for growth in poorer countries and communities. Similarly, there does not appear to be any conflict between basic needs and political rights as those developing countries enjoying greater political rights and civil liberties also performed better, with some exceptions, in terms of life expectancy, infant survival rates and per capita incomes.

Basic education, especially of women, has emerged as the single highest priority in most studies of basic needs performance. Not only are basic literacy and numeracy key instruments for acquiring new knowledge and productive skills, but they are also essential for full political participation and personal development. High rates of literacy coincided with the beginning of large-scale struggles for rights in nineteenth-century Europe (Howard 1989)

The fact that malnutrition has multiple origins means that a range of measures is required to address the problem. Raising the incomes of vulnerable groups must be part of the solution but, for most of the poorer countries, the growth of the economy as a whole is unlikely to be sufficient to provide significant alleviation of malnutrition in the short to medium term (Stern 1989). Public intervention is called for to protect the incomes, or at least consumption levels, of the most vulnerable groups. Nutritional well-being can also be enhanced by the provision of education and health services, sanitation and water supply – all of which may be more efficiently and equitably supplied through the public sector.

There is also a need to alter some of the ethical notions of right and wrong which lie at the heart of public policies. There is a widely held belief that "to produce is virtuous; to produce food is considered exceptionally virtuous; and to receive entitlements or to augment the purchasing power in the market of those who earn less than what they need is sinful" (Reutlinger, quoted in LeMay 1988). Thus, the subsidisation of production (and stocks) is perceived as just – a reward for hardworking citizens – while the subsidisation of consumption is perceived as relief and welfare for the unworthy.

Participation

The human element of basic needs/rights, and indeed of development as a whole, can be ensured only through the participation of peoples/communities in decisions and actions affecting their lives. Participation has at least three positive functions to play as a vital component of development strategy (Goulet 1989):

1) it guarantees government's non-instrumental treatment of powerless people by bringing them dignity as beings of worth;

2) it serves as a valuable instrument for mobilising, organising and promoting action by people themselves as the major problem solvers in their social environment; and

3) it functions as a channel through which local communities or movements gain access to larger, macro arenas of decision-making.

In most developing countries, it is the NGOs who have done most to further the cause of participation in both theory and practice. The organisations which have been most successful in stimulating broad and sustained processes of participation have generally been those whose members could expect some material benefits from their efforts. In particular, the success of participation has frequently depended on the capacity of grass-roots organisations to demand and obtain certain services which only the state apparatus could provide (Prealc 1987). In this context, the struggle for basic needs/rights could provide one strong issue around which mobilisation might be successfully organised.

Conclusions

The plight of the global poor is the worst offence against basic rights in contemporary world society—the alleviation of their condition deserves to be the first priority. However, the satisfaction even of basic needs would be permanently achievable "only with structural changes at all levels, local, national and international, that would enable those concerned to identify their own needs, mobilise their own resources and shape their future in their own terms" (International Commission of Jurists 1981).

The adoption of the UN Covenant on Economic, Social and Cultural Rights, and its subsequent ratification by the majority of UN members, establishes basic needs as human rights in a legal sense. Before they can become meaningful as human rights, it will be necessary to achieve international agreement on definitions and indicators and then to generate mechanisms for recording relevant aspects of human wellbeing on a disaggregated basis (Stewart 1988). As regards actual implementation, it would seem preferable to focus on a core group of rights (civil/political as well as subsistence), to establish country-specific thresholds and to strive for their fulfilment as an essential prerequisite for the progressive achievement of the full human rights standards.

Human rights institutions in most of the "like-minded' countries (the Nordic countries, Canada and the Netherlands) now cooperate to produce an annual account of the human rights situation in those developing countries with which they have close relationships (e.g. Nowak and Swinehart 1989). Now that Ireland has ratified the UN covenants, it would be possible and desirable for it to join this effort.

"The meeting of basic needs would not deliver freedom for the poor, any more than the abolition of the slave trade gave the slaves their liberty, but both are prerequisites of freedom" (Vincent 1986). The achievement of such basic rights would not be a mere palliative as it would eliminate some obstacles impeding authentic development and create new possibilities of moving towards the eventual achievement of such development. Thus, the addressing of basic rights on a participative basis could be the initial step in a broader improvement and empowerment process.

Bread and Freedom

Bibliography

Ardalla, I-S. (1986), "Needs and desires: a new approach to consumption analysis", *Development and Peace*, 7(1)

Adedeji, A. (1989), Foreword to ECA (1989) op. cit.

Adelman, I. (1986), "A poverty-focussed approach to development policy", in J.P. Lewis and V. Kallab (eds) *Development Policies Reconsidered*, Transaction Books (for Overseas Development Council)

Adelman, I. and C.T. Morris (1973), *Economic Growth and Social Equity in Developing Countries*, Stanford University Press

Alston P. (1979) "Human rights and the basic needs strategy for development" *Human Rights and Development Working Paper*, London, Anti-Slavery Society

Alston, P. (1981), "Prevention versus cure as a human rights strategy", in International Commission of Jurists (1981) op. cit.

Alston, P. (1987), "Out of the abyss: the challenges confronting the new U.N. Committee on Economic, Social and Cultural Rights", *Human Rights Quarterly*, 9 (3)

Andreassen, B-A. and A. Eide (eds) (1988), *Human Rights in Developing Countries 1987/88*, Copenhagen, Akademisk Vorlag

Andreassen, B-A. T., Skalnes, A.G. Smith and H. Stokke (1988), "Assessing human rights performance in developing countries: the case for a minimal threshold approach to economic and social rights", in Andreassen and Eide (1988) op. cit.

Anon (1982), *Report on Development Cooperation and Human Rights*, (Rapporteur: Mr. Holtz), Doc. 4997, Parliamentary Assembly of the Council of Europe

Behrman, J.R., A.B. Deolalikar, and B.L. Wolfe (1988), "Nutrients: impacts and determinants", *World Bank Economic Review*, 2 (3)

Bertrand, C. (1985), "Some reflections on reform of the United Nations", *UN Joint Inspection Unit Report* No. 85/9, New York, UN Doc. No. A/40/988.

Bhagwati, J.N. (1988), "Poverty and public policy", *World Development*, 16 (5)

Brodhead, T. (1987), "NGOs: in one year, out the other?", *World Development*, 15 (S)

Burki, S.J. (1980), "Sectoral priorities for meeting basic needs", in *Poverty and Basic Needs*, Washington DC, World Bank.

Burki, S.J. and M. Ul Haq (1981), "Meeting basic needs: an overview", *World Development*, 9 (2)

Caldwell, J.C. (1986), "Routes to low mortality in developing countries", *Population and Development Review*, 12 (2)

Chenery, H.B., M.S. Ahluwalia, C.L.G. Bell, J.H. Duloy, and R. Jolly (1974), *Redistribution with Growth: An Approach to Policy*, Oxford University Press

Clark, J. (1988), Debt and Poverty: *A Case Study of Zambia*, Oxford, Oxfam

Cleland, J. and J. Van Ginneken (1989), "Maternal schooling and childhood mortality", *Journal of Biological Science*, Supplement No. 10.

Cohen, S. (1986), "A comparative study of needs and their satisfaction", *E.A.D.I. Bulletin* 1.86

Coomaraswamy, R. (1982), "A third world view of human rights", *UNESCO Courier*, Aug-Sept 1982.

Cornia, G.A. (1984), "A summary and interpretation of the evidence" in Jolly and Cornia op. cit.

Cornia, G.A. (1987), "Economic decline and human welfare in the first half of the 1980s", in Cornia et al, op.cit.

Cornia, G.A., R. Jolly and F. Stewart (1987), *Adjustment with a Human Face*, Oxford, Oxford University Press

Croll, E. (1986), *Food Supply in China and the Nutritional Status of Children*, U.N. Research Institute for Social Development, Geneva

Dasgupta, P. (1989), "Well-being and the extent of its realisation in poor countries", *Discussion Paper* No. 19, Development Economics Research Programme, London School of Economics

Dell, S. (1979), "Basic needs in comprehensive development: should the UNDP have a development strategy?", *World Development*, 7 (3)

De Kadt, E. (1980), "Some basic questions of human rights and development", *World Development*, 8 (2)

Dias, C.J. (1981), "Realizing the right to development: The importance of legal resources" in International Commission of Jurists op. cit.

Dias, C.J. (1984), "The legal resources approach" in Eide et al, op. cit.

Donnelly, J. (1982), "Human rights and human dignity: An analytical critique of non-western conceptions of human rights", *The American Political Science Review*, 76 (2)

ECA, (1989), *African Alternative Framework to Structural Adjustment Programmes for Socio-Economic Recovery and Transformation*, Addis Ababa, Economic Commission for Africa

Egeland, J. (1988), "Strengthening the first line of defence: Third World human rights groups", in Andressen and Eide op. cit.

Eide, A. (1989), "Realization of social and economic rights and the minimum threshold approach", *Human Rights Law Journal* 10 (1/2)

Eide, A. et al [eds] (1984), *Food as a Human Right*, Tokyo, United Nations University

FAO, (1985), *The Fifth World Food Survey*, Rome, Food and Agriculture Organisation of the UN

FAO (1987) *Agriculture Towards 2000*, Rome, Food and Agriculture Organisation of the UN

FAO (1990) *Production Yearbook, No. 43*, Rome, Food and Agriculture Organisation of the UN

Fishlow, A. (1984), "Comments", *World Development*, 12 (9).

Forsythe, D.P. (ed) (1989), *Human Rights and Development: International Views*, London, Macmillan

Friedmann, J. (1979), "Basic needs, agropolitan development and planning from below", *World Development*, 7 (6)

Galtung, J. (1978), "Grand designs on a collision course", *International Development Review*, 3-4

Goldstein, J.S. (1985), "Basic human needs: the plateau curve" *World Development*, 13 (5)

Goulet, D. (1989), "Participation in development: new avenues" *World Development*, 17 (2)

Grant, J.P. (1973), "Development: the end of trickle down", Foreign Policy, 12

Grant, J.P. (1989), Preface to UNICEF (1989) op. cit.

Haq Ul, M. (1981), Foreword to Streeten et al, op. cit.

Hebel von, H. (1989), "The concept of development: from economics to human rights", Background Paper for FONDAD Conference: "Towards European Action on Debt, 21-2 March 1989, The Hague

Hicks, N. (1979), "Growth vs basic needs: is there a trade-off?", *World Development*, 7 (11/12)

Hicks, N. (1982), "Sector priorities in meeting basic needs: some statistical evidence", *World Development*, 10 (6)

Hicks N. and P. Streeten (1979), "Indicators of development: the search for a basic needs yardstick", *World Development* 7 (6)

Hopkins, M. and R. Van Der Hoeven (1983), *Basic Needs in Development Planning*, Gower (for ILO)

Howard, R.E. (1989), "Human rights development and foreign policy", in Forsythe op. cit.

ILO (1976), *Employment, Growth and Basic Needs, A One World Problem*, Geneva International Labour Organisation

International Commission of Jurists (1981), *Development, Human Rights and the Rule of Law*, Pergamon

Isenman, P. (1987), "A comment on 'growth and equity in developing countries: a reinterpretation of the Sri Lankan experience' by Bhalla and Glewwe", *World Bank Economic Review*, 1(3)

Jhabvala, F. (1984), "On human rights and the socio-economic context", *Netherlands International Law Review*, 31

Jolly, R. (1976), "The world employment conference: the enthronement of basic needs", *ODI Review*, No.2

Jolly R. and G.A. Cornia (eds.) (1984), *The Impact of World Recession on Children*, Pergamon (for UNICEF)

Korten, D.C. (1987), "Third generation NGO strategies: a key to people-centred development", *World Development*, 15 (S)

Kothari, S. (1989), "The human rights movement in India: crisis and challenges", in Forsythe op. cit.

Kung, H. and J. Moltmann (eds) (1990), *The Ethics of World Religions and Human Rights*, London, SCM Press

Kuznets, S. (1955), "Economic growth and income inequality", *American Economic Review*, 45

Kuznets, S. (1963), "Quantitative aspects of economic growth of nations: V111, Distribution of income by size", *Economic Development and Cultural Change*, 11 (2)

Leipziger, D.M. and M.A. Lewis (1980), "Social indicators, growth and distribution", *World Development*, 8 (4)

Le May, B.W.J. (1988) [ed], *Science, Ethics and Food*, Washington, Smithsonian Institution Press

Lipton, M. (1988), "The poor and the poorest: some interim findings", *World Bank Discussion Paper No. 25*, Washington D.C.

Lisk, F. (1985), "Conventional development strategies and basic needs fulfilment: A reassessment of objectives and policies", *International Labour Review*, 115 (2)

Maduagwu, M.O. (1987), *Ethical Relativism versus Human Rights*, Vienna, International Progress Organisation

Maizels, A. and M.K. Nissanke (1984), "Motivations for aid to developing countries", *World Development*, 12 (9)

Martin, E.M. (1985), "Jobs and other basic needs", in OECD, *Twenty-five Years of Development Cooperation: A Review*, Paris

Maslow, A.H. (1968), *Towards a Psychology of Being* (2nd edn.) New York D. Van Nostrand Co.

Maslow, A.H. (1987), *Motivation and Personality* (3rd edn.) New York, Harper and Row,

Moltmann, J. (1990), *"Human rights, the rights of humanity and the rights of nature"*, in Kung and Moltmann op. cit.

Morawetz, D. (1977), *Twenty-five Years of Economic Development 1950 to 1975*, Washington D.C., World Bank

Morris, M.D. (1970), *Measuring the Condition of the World's Poor*, Pergamon (for Overseas Development Council)

Naiken, L. (1988), "Comparison of the FAO and World Bank methodology for estimating the incidence of undernutrition", *FAO Quarterly Bulletin of Statistics*, 1 (3)

Newman, B.A. and R.J. Thomson (1989), "Economic growth and social development: a longitudinal analysis of causal priority", *World Development*, 17 (4)

Nissan and Caveney (1988), "Relative welfare improvements of low income versus high income countries", *World Development*, 16 (5)

Nolan, B. (1990), Report Review, *Trócaire Development Review 1990*, Dublin

Nowak, M. and T. Swinehart (eds) (1989), *Human Rights in Developing Countries 1989*, Kehl am Rhein, N.P. Engel

ODI (1988), "The rich and the poor: changes in incomes of developing countries since 1960", Briefing Paper, June 1988 London, Overseas Development Institute

ODI (1988a), "NGOs in Development", Briefing Paper, August 1988, London, Overseas Development Institute

OECD (1976), "Measuring social well-being: a progress report on the development of social indicators", Paris, OECD

OECD (Various), "Development Co-operation: efforts and policies of the members of the Development Assistance Committee", Paris, Organisation for Economic Cooperation and Development

Opsahl, T. (1989), "Instruments of implementation of human rights", *Human Rights Law Journal*, 10 (1/2).

Pfeffermann, G. (1987), "Economic crisis and the poor in some Latin American countries", *Finance and Development*, June 1987

Pinstrup-Andersen P., M. Jaramillo and F. Stewart (1987), "The impact on government expenditure", in Cornia et al, op. cit.

Prealc (1987), *In Search of Equity: Planning for the Satisfaction of Basic Needs in Latin America*, Aldershot, Averbury

Pritchard, K. (1989), *"Human Rights and Development: Theory and Data"*, in Forsythe op. cit.

Reutlinger, S. and H. Alderman (1980), "The prevalence of calorie-deficient diets in developing countries", *World Development*, 8 (5/6)

Reynolds, J. (1983), "The spread of economic growth to the Third World: 1850-1980", *Journal of Economic Literature*, 21

Rubin, B.R. (1989), "Human Rights and Development: Reflections on Social Movements in India", in Forsythe (1989) op. cit.

Sahn, D.E. (1987), "Changes in the living standards of the poor in Sri Lanka during a period of macroeconomic restructuring", *World Development*, 15 (6)

Sahn, D.E. and H. Alderman (1988), "The effects of human capital on wages and the determinants of labor supply in a developing country", *Journal of Development Econmics*, 29 (2)

Saksena, K.P. (1989), "Human rights and development: an Asian perspective", Forword to Forsythe (1989) op. cit.

Sangmeister H. (1987), "Economic growth or the satisfaction of basic needs: false alternatives for sub-Saharan Africa", *Economics*, 36

Selowsky, M. (1987), "Adjustment in the 1980s: an overview of issues", *Finance and Development*, June 1987

Sen, A.K. (1981), "Public action and the quality of life in developing countries", *Oxford Bulletin of Economics and Statistics*, 43

Sen, A.K. (1984), *Resources, Values and Development*, Oxford, Blackwell

Sen, A. (1987), *Hunger and Entitlements*, Helsinki, World Institute for Development Economics Research

Shue, H. (1980), *Basic Rights: Subsistence, Affluence and U.S. Foreign Policy*, Princeton University Press

Singh, A. (1979), "The basic needs approach to development vs the new international economic order: the significance of Third World industrialization", *World Development*, 7 (6)

Sivard, R.L. (1983), *World Military and Social Expenditures 1983/84*, Washington D.C., World Priorities

Sivard, R.L. (1987), *World Military and Social Expenditures 1987/88*, Washington D.C., World Priorities.

Stern, N. (1989), "The economics of development: a survey", *The Economic Journal*, 99

Stewart, F. (1985), *Planning To Meet Basic Needs*, London, Macmillan

Stewart, F. (1988), "Basic needs strategies, human rights and the right to development", *Ld'A-QEH Development Studies Working Papers* No. 2

Strauss, J. (1986), "Does better nutrition raise farm productivity?", *Journal of Political Economy*, 94 (2)

Streeten, P. (1984), "Basic needs: some unsettled questions", *World Development*, 12 (9)

Streeten, P. and S.J. Burki (1978), "Basic needs: some issues", *World Development*, 6 (3)

Streeten, P., J. Burki, M. Ul Haq, N. Hicks and F. Stewart (1981) *First Things First: Meeting Basic Needs in Developing Countries*, World Bank and Oxford University Press

Taylor, C.L. and D.A. Jodice (1983), *World Handbook of Political and Social Indicators*, Yale University Press

Toye, J. (1987), *Dilemmas of Development*, Longmans, London.

Trivedi, R.W. (1981), "Human rights, right to development and the new international economic order - perspectives and proposals", in International Commission of Jurists (1981), op. cit.

UNCTAD (1988), *Handbook of International Trade and Development Statistics*, New York, United Nations

UNCTAD (1989), *Trade and Development Report 1989*, New York, United Nations

UNDP (1990), *Human Development Report 1990*, New York, Oxford University Press

UNDP (1991), *Human Development Report 1991*, New York, Oxford University Press

UNECA (1988), *Survey of Economic and Social Conditions in Africa 1985/86*, New York, United Nations

UNICEF (1989), *The State of the World's Children 1989*, Oxford, Oxford University Press

UNICEF (1991), *The State of the World's Children 1991*, Oxford, Oxford University Press

UNIDO (1984), *Industrialization and Social Development*, 1960-1980, Vienna, UNIDO/IS 441

United Nations (1988), *Mortality of Children Under Age 5: World Estimates and Projections 1950-2025*, New York, United Nations

van Boven, T (1989), "Human Rights and Development: The UN Experience", in Forsythe (1989), op. cit.

Vincent, R.J. (1986), *Human Rights and International Relations*, Cambridge University Press (in association with the Royal Institute of International Affairs)

Walf, K. (1990), "Gospel, Church Law and Human Rights: Foundations and Deficiences", in Kung and Moltmann op. cit.

Weigel, V.B. (1986), "The basic needs approach: overcoming the poverty of homo economicus", *World Development*, 14 (12)

Wiedemann, P. and K. Muller (1984), "Socio-economic development in the newly industrialising countries", *Labour and Society*, 9 (3)

Wijkman, A. and L. Timberlake (1984), *Natural Disasters: Acts of God or Acts of Man*, London, Earthscan

Wisner, B. (1988), *Power and Need in Africa: Basic Human Needs and Development Policies*, London, Earthscan

Wolfe, B.L. and J.B. Behrman (1982), "The determinants of child mortality, health and nutrition in a developing country", *Journal of Development Economics*, 11 (2)

Wood, R.E. (1986), *From Marshall Plan to Debt Crisis: Foreign Aid and Development Choices in the World Economy*, Berkely, University of California Press

Wood, R.H. (1988), "Literacy and basic needs satisfaction in Mexico", *World Development*, 16 (3)

World Bank (1980), *Education Sector Policy Paper*, Washington D.C.

World Bank (1986), *Poverty and Hunger: Issues and Options for Food Security in Developing Countries*, Washington D.C.

World Bank (1987), "Protecting the poor during periods of adjustment", Background Paper for Development Countries, Washington, D.C.

World Bank (1989), *Sub-Saharan Africa: From Crisis to Sustainable Growth*, Washington D.C.

World Bank (Various), *World Development Reports*, Washington

Zacaquette, J. (1984), "The relationship between development and human rights", in Eide et al.(1984), op.cit.

Bread and Freedom

Index

official aid 23-4
oral rehydration therapy 55
Organisation for Economic
    Cooperation and Development
    16, 21, 23, 40
Organisation of African Unity 69

Pakistan 18, 29, 60
participation 85-6
Peru 49
Philippines 25, 29
Physical Quality of Life Index
    (PQLI) 40-2
political poverty 52
population growth 26

Red Crescent 51
Red Cross 51
redistribution with growth 27, 35
refugees 11
rights of solidarity 65
Rwanda 51

Saudi Arabia 16
Second Development Decade 26
Sierra Leone 44, 45, 51, 57
Singapore 16, 18
slavery 86
soft loans 16
Somalia 42, 44
South Africa 59
South Korea 16, 18, 59
Spain 16
Sri Lanka 11, 12, 42, 54, 57, 59,
    60
Sub-Saharan Africa 11, 19, 20,
    51, 54, 77, 82
Sudan 16
Sweden 22, 42

Taiwan 59
Tanzania 17, 24, 26, 42, 51, 54,
    55
Thailand 42

Third World Forum 83
trickle-down 25-6, 35, 58
trickle-up 58
Turkey 16

U-5 mortality (see infant
    mortality)
UN Centre for Human Rights 71
UN Charter 71
UN Development Programme 42,
    62, 64, 72
UN Economic and Social
    Committee 72
UNESCO (UN Education
    Scientific and Cultural
    Organisation 50, 71-2
UN General Assembly 26, 28, 30,
    37, 66
UN Human Rights Committee
    72
UNICEF (UN Children's Fund):
    adjustment 10, 31-2, 82;
    Covenants 71;
    human needs costs 81-2;
    malnutrition 48; public
    spending 54;
    U-5 mortality 42
UN Industrial Development
    Organisation 83
UN Joint Inspection Unit 71
United Arab Emirates 16
United States: Charter of Alliance
    for Progress 25; economic
    output 17;
    Human Development Index
    42; overseas aid 22, 23; UN
    votes 66
Universal Declaration of Human
    Rights 12, 65
US Agency for International
    Development (USAID) 26
USSR 21, 68

Venezuela 16

Bread and Freedom